WriteGuide's Individualized Spelling Program

By Benjamin Ludwig

Copyright © June, 2000
http://www.writeguide.com

ISBN 1-886061-25-4

A Quick Note from the Author…

Dear Reader,

I was a terrible speller when I was in school. I went through phonics programs, took all sorts of tests, tried all sorts of exercises, and nothing worked.

As I got older, I found ways to deal with the problem. Spell checkers work wonderfully, and there are lots of little tips and tricks that can help as well. The problem is that all those things take up too much time. Some of the spelling rules I learned along the way worked pretty well, but many of them were just plain confusing. For example, you know that /i/ before /e/, except after /c/ rule. Well, how about the words *height* and *foreign*? And what about *beige*, *seize*, or *heifer*?

I knew that if I was ever going to become a good speller, I needed to come up with something new. And I knew there were lots of other people out there who had the same problem. So I made a decision: I decided to design an individualized spelling program that could help people spell any word in the English language, no matter how complicated the word might be.

That was over a year ago.

The manual you're holding in your hands right now works. It won't take you long to figure out how to use it. The exercises it will ask you to do are easy. There aren't any long lists of words to memorize, and there aren't any tests. All it takes to be successful with this program is the ability to look things up in a dictionary, the willingness to write a few things down in a notebook, and the ability to say, "Mom, can you circle all the spelling errors in my paper?"

That's all I have to say for now, so I'll end here. Enjoy the program, and if you're ever online feel free to drop me a quick e-mail.

Sincerely,

Benjamin Ludwig
Ludwig@writeguide.com

Table of Contents

Individual Word Lists:

Introduction

English is an amazingly versatile, powerful language – but its spelling is downright difficult. It's based on rules, but almost all the rules have exceptions. It's based on specific sounds, but almost all the sounds can be produced by several different letters and letter combinations. The result is that native speakers are often awful spellers.

Today with spellcheckers on computers and other electronic devices, many folks would like to just leave it to the electronics. This is not the ultimate solution either as the poem below shows.

Ode to the Spell Checker

I have a spelling checker.
It came with my PC.
It plane lee marks four my revue,
Miss steaks aye can knot sea.

Eye ran this poem threw it,
Your sure reel glad two no.
Its vary polished in its weigh,
My checker tolled me sew.

A checker is a bless sing,
It freeze yew lodes of thyme.
It helps me right awl stiles two reed,
And aides me when aye rime.

To rite with care is quite a feet,
Of which won should be proud.
And wee mussed dew the best we can,
Sew flaws are knot aloud.

And now bee cause my spelling,
Is checked with such grate flare,
Their are know faults with in my cite,
Of none eye am a wear.

Each frays come posed up on my screen,
Eye trussed to bee a joule,
The checker poured o'er every word,
To cheque sum spelling rule.

That's why aye brake in two averse,
By righting wants too pleas,
Sow now ewe sea why aye dew prays,
Such soft wear for pea seas!

Mechanical devices are a help, but they are not the ultimate solution. It's obviously best to know how to spell correctly. How to achieve such mastery is the problem. There are ways to deal with this problem. You can memorize spelling rules and all their exceptions. You can study long lists of words and eventually memorize all the words you need to know how to spell. You can and should use the dictionary when needed. You can use a spell checker, but remember the limitations as seen in the poem above.

What most people don't realize is that there's something far more efficient than memorizing rules, exceptions, and lists; there's *phonetic spelling*. Phonetic spelling is what you find in the dictionary. It's made up of 21 consonants and lots of strange-looking vowels with funny marks and symbols all over them. Although there are a lot of different *phonetic symbols*, there's nothing inherently confusing about any of them. There are no special rules that govern them; thus, there are no exceptions. A phonetic symbol is a phonetic symbol, and for the most part will never be pronounced any differently.

Here's the important part: if you can identify a group of words that are spelled the same, **not only in terms of their English spelling but also in terms of their phonetic spelling,** your brain can group them all together and automatically memorize the spelling.

I'll give you an example. Let's say you were trying to spell the word *pear*, but instead you spelled it *pare*. That's a reasonable mistake to make, isn't it? They're both legitimate words, and according to the rules of phonics they're pronounced the same. If you were to look up the word *pear* in the dictionary you'd see that its phonetic pronunciation is /pâr/. Strangely enough, the word *dare* also has an /âr/ in it, as do the words *hair* and *aerial*. In fact, the only **phonetic** difference between *pear*, *dare*, and *hair* is the first letter in each word, and yet every single one of them is spelled differently.

So if someone gave you a long list of words that contain the phonetic combination /âr/, you wouldn't be able to find any recognizable patterns. You wouldn't know whether to spell *pear* with an *e-a-r* an *a-r-e*, an *a-i-r*, or an *a-e-r*. The phonetic spellings and the English spellings are completely different from one another.

The most efficient way to remember how to spell *pear* with an *e-a-r* is to find other words that have the same **phonetic** spelling as the word *pear*, that is, a list of words in which the **phonetic spelling must match the English spelling**. Some examples include *bear*, *swear*, and *wear*.

However, coming up with those three words isn't nearly as easy as you might think. If you could somehow find a list of words that contain the /ear/ spelling, you'd find words such as *hear*, *heart*, *ear*, and *earn* – none of which are pronounced like the word *pear*. And if you could find a list of words that contain the phonetic /âr/ sound, you'd find words like *dare*, *hair*, *aerial*, *where*, and *their* – none of which have the same English spelling. No wonder spelling is such an issue for so many people!

In order to do away with all the confusion, **we've done something that's never been done before**: we've identified, categorized, and cross-referenced all the sound/letter patterns in the English language, and provided a list of examples for all of them. Using the lists in conjunction with some simple memorization techniques will enable you to correctly spell all the words that you'd ordinarily misspell. It's a simple concept based on the reliable, common sense principle that patterns and examples are easier to memorize than a long list of rules and their individual exceptions.

How to Use WriteGuide's Individualized Spelling Program

This manual was designed to be used by people of all ages, and should last a lifetime. It's written directly to student, but it's expected that parents will read through quite a bit of it as well. In order to use it you need three important things: a dictionary that contains phonetic spellings, a blank notebook, and some method of figuring out which words you misspell in your writing. The dictionary is needed because the phonetic spellings listed in it will allow you to identify whichever Word Lists are necessary to eliminate your spelling errors. The notebook is important because you need a place where you can practice some important exercises. To figure out which words you're misspelling in your writing, you should have someone take a look at your paper and circle all the errors. That person will most likely be a parent or teacher, but older siblings or friends work just as well if they happen to be a better speller than you are. If you use a word processor to type your work, you should turn the spell checker OFF and print out a finished copy so that someone can go through it to find your errors.

This brings us to two important points, namely **1) this program isn't designed to teach people how to read,** and **2) it assumes its students have a fair degree of reading/decoding skills.** By "fair degree of reading/decoding skills," I mean the student should be able to read at least on a second or third grade level. Students who use the program should be able to read a wide variety of basic words and should be capable of looking words up in a dictionary; at least they should be ready to begin learning how to do so. Older students, say age 13 and higher, should be able to use the program without any help at all. Younger students, those age 12 and younger, could probably use the help of a parent or teacher. If you're not sure whether or not someone can handle the program on his own, let him try it out. The results will make the decision for you.

As I mentioned before, this program doesn't involved pre-packaged lists of spelling words that must be memorized according to age and ability levels. Instead it draws its words entirely from the student's writing, using carefully designed memory techniques to ingrain certain spelling patterns in his or her mind. It's an entirely new paradigm for teaching spelling and was designed to bypass all the complex, confusing rules of traditional spelling systems.

In order to use the program, you need to understand that the English language is made up of a set of phonetic symbols which are used to help people pronounce its words. Below is a list of all the symbols used in the manual. You'll find similar lists in the beginning of most dictionaries. Next to each symbol is a word in which the symbol is represented in **bold** print. Some of the sounds change slightly when you use them in different words, but the difference is so slight it isn't worth mentioning. When you start using the program, you'll have no trouble recognizing any of them no matter where they appear.

Pronunciation Key

ā	age	ō	zone
ă	apple	ŏ	box
â	area	o͞o	boot
ä	calm	o͝o	good
b	boy	p	pay
ch	chair	r	rock
d	dog	s	sight
ē	even	sh	show
ĕ	beg	t	tap
f	for	th	think
g	God	ŭ	tub
h	how	û	work
ī	dive	v	van
ĭ	big	w	way
î	pier	y	yes
j	jam	z	zoo
k	kite	zh	garage, pleasure
l	love	ə	moral, physician, asparagus
m	man		
ng	thing		

The bulk of this manual is divided into lots of different Word Lists, all of which are alphabetized and broken down into different Sub-Lists. You can tell a Word List when you see one because it will state a specific letter of the alphabet followed by a number. An example would be "A-15" or "X-2." Sub-Lists are very different from Word Lists. Sub-Lists give you specific letter patterns that cause errors. Sub-Lists are always listed in lowercase letters. For example, /ib/, /le/, and /ao/ are all Sub-Lists within different Word Lists. Referring someone to Sub-List /ib/ would therefore be confusing because Word Lists I-1, I-2, and I-3 all contain Sub-Lists labeled /ib/. Specifically, Word Lists refer to sounds created by a letter or letter pattern while Sub-Lists refer to sounds created by letters or letter patterns **and** the letter or letters directly preceding or following them.

Take a look at this example from page 30 and you'll see exactly what I'm talking about.

List A-23
(/ar/ pronounced /âr/ with no silent /e/ ending)
The sound /a/ as spelled and pronounced in the words

"caramel" and "daring"

---

ara	caramel, caravan, marathon, parachute, paradise, paragraph, parakeet
are	area, Jared
ari	caribou, caring, daring, garish, garrison, marigold, mariner, snaring, staring

---

So you get a paper with lots of misspelled words, all of which are identified and circled. What do you do next? In the next few pages there are some very specific directions to follow, but I'll give a brief summary right here.

When you identify a misspelled word, you'll do five things: 1) look it up in the dictionary, 2) identify the phonetic spelling, 3) look up the phonetic spelling in the Word Lists, 4) add your error to the Word List, and 5) practice a few simple exercises that will guarantee you never misspell the word again.

There are three official stages to using *WriteGuide's Individualized Spelling Program*, each of which is made up of a series of smaller steps. The first stage, called **Identification**, involves identifying not only words that are spelled wrong but also the specific letter/sound pattern that causes the error. Identification is just about impossible without the phonetic spellings listed in your dictionary. Before beginning the Identification stage, someone else, and this is where moms, dads, and teachers come in, must proofread your paper, circling or marking all the spelling errors. From there it's just a matter of using the three stages to go through one word at a time.

The second stage, called **Preparation**, involves looking through the various Word Lists and Sub-Lists. Once you find the right ones, you'll be asked to pick some words which will be used in the third stage. The words you are picking out are **practice words**, and you'll find out all about those shortly.

Stage three is called **The Exercise**, and it involves something called the **Primary Exercise**. It is primary not only because it's the first exercise you'll do, but it's also the most important. You'll find a practice Primary Exercise sheet on **page 14**which may be photocopied and reproduced by the purchaser or owner of the program. On **page 15** you'll find a **Notebook Template**, which also may be reproduced and used in place of a notebook. These sheets may be used to keep a record of the words you learn. Also, studying the two sheets will help guide you through the three stages of the program.

The Three Stages

Stage One

Identification (Steps 1-7, to be completed in the student's notebook, or on a Notebook Template Sheet.)

1. Write the number "1" in your notebook, and then write the sentence containing your spelling error. This will be your **Original Sentence**. Make sure the misspelled word remains misspelled. Then identify the misspelled word by underlining or circling it.

2. Write the number "2" in your notebook. Look up the correct spelling in the dictionary and write it down. This will be your **Primary Word**. If you want, you can even label it "Primary Word."

3. Write the number "3" in your notebook. Compare the phonetic spelling in the dictionary to the spelling in your **Primary Word**, and figure out which letter or letters in your **Primary Word** caused you to spell the word wrong. When you find them, write them down. This will be your **Error-Causer**. Again, you can label it by writing "Error-Causer" on the same line.

    (If you find that a particular word contains more than one **Error-Causer**, simply go through these directions twice, once with each **Error-Causer**. Just make sure your **Primary Word** is always spelled correctly.)

4. Write the number "4" in your notebook. Using the **Primary Word's** phonetic spelling as listed in the dictionary, write down the phonetic symbol that takes the place of the **Error-Causer**. This is called your **Phonetic Pattern**. If you want, you can label it.

5. Write the number "5" in your notebook. Then write your **Error-Causer**, followed by the word *pronounced*, and then the **Phonetic Pattern** identified in Step 4. This is your **Word List Phrase**. This is so that the format used in your notebook will match the pronounced format used throughout the manual. The examples on **page 7** will help explain.

    If your **Error-Causer** happens to be a silent letter, simply write *silent e* or *silent u* in your notebook instead of *pronounced*. Take a look through some of the Word Lists for some examples; silent letters are listed at the end of each Word List.

6. Write the number "6" in your notebook. Using the Word Lists, find the list of words that best matches whatever phrase happens to be on line 5. Write the title of the Word List in your notebook, and then enter your **Primary Word** into the manual. Write it in one of the blanks within the Word List you just found.

    If you can't find a Word List for your **Primary Word** or your dictionary lists more than one pronunciation of your **Primary Word**, go to **Step 12**, entitled **"Desperate Measures"** on **page 10**.

7. Write the number "7" in your notebook. Within the Word List, identify the Sub-List which best categorizes your **Error-Causer** and write it in your notebook. It may be necessary to add a letter to the beginning or end of your **Error-Causer** so that it matches the Sub-List perfectly.

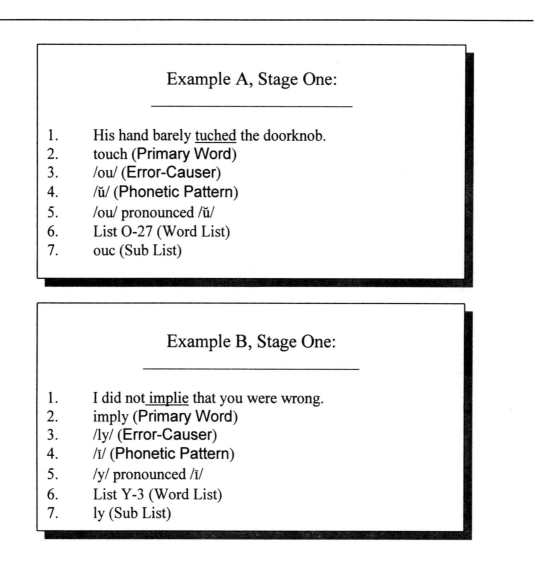

Example A, Stage One:

1. His hand barely <u>tuched</u> the doorknob.
2. touch (Primary Word)
3. /ou/ (Error-Causer)
4. /ŭ/ (Phonetic Pattern)
5. /ou/ pronounced /ŭ/
6. List O-27 (Word List)
7. ouc (Sub List)

Example B, Stage One:

1. I did not <u>implie</u> that you were wrong.
2. imply (Primary Word)
3. /ly/ (Error-Causer)
4. /ī/ (Phonetic Pattern)
5. /y/ pronounced /ī/
6. List Y-3 (Word List)
7. ly (Sub List)

Stage Two
Preparation (Step 8, to be completed in the student's notebook.)

8. Write the number "8" in your notebook. Look through the Sub-List to see whether or not you can already spell any of the words. If you can in fact spell some of them, choose the two that seem easiest, and write them down in your notebook. These will be your **Practice Words**, and you can move on to **Step 11**. If you can't spell any of the words, see **Step 8A**. If there are less than three words in the list, see **Step 8B**.

8A. If you can't spell any of the words in the list, choose two that you think might be easiest to learn. Write them down in your notebook. These will be your **Practice Words**. Underline the **Error-Causer** in each of them, and proceed to **Step 9**.

8B. If there are less than three words in the list and you can't spell them, look for other Word Lists that deal with the same **Error-Causer**. Within those lists (there will probably be several), look for words that contain the same **Letter Pattern** but are pronounced differently. Of those words, choose two that you consider to be particularly easy to spell. Write them down in your notebook. These will be your **Practice Words**. Underline the **Error-Causer** in each of them, and proceed to **Step 9**. Then, when you finish steps 1-11, practice the **Rhyme, Rhyme, NOT QUITE Rhyme** exercise listed in the **Additional Exercises** section on **page 12**.

If there are still no other Word Lists that contain the letter pattern you need, see **Step 12** **(found on page 10).**

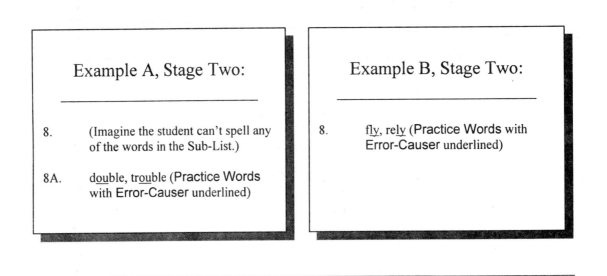

Example A, Stage Two:	Example B, Stage Two:
8. (Imagine the student can't spell any of the words in the Sub-List.)	8. fl<u>y</u>, rel<u>y</u> (Practice Words with Error-Causer underlined)
8A. d<u>ou</u>ble, tr<u>ou</u>ble (Practice Words with Error-Causer underlined)	

Stage Three

The Exercise (Steps 9-11, to be completed in the student's notebook.)

Note: The **Primary Exercise** may be repeated periodically as needed, in order to help refresh the student's memory.

9. Write the number "9" in your notebook. Then write down your **Primary Word**, followed by your two **Practice Words**. Underline all three **Error-Causers** as you write the words. DO NOT wait until you finish writing each word to underline the **Error-Causer**, and DO NOT wait until you finish writing all three.

10. Write the number "10" in your notebook. Using the three words, create a sentence. This sentence is your **Primary Sentence**. Modifying the words (i.e. adding an /ed/, an /ing/, or an /s/ ending) is acceptable. Write the sentence three times. Underline the **Error-Causers** as you write them. Read the sentences out loud as you write them, emphasizing the **Error-Causer**.

11. Write the number "11" in your notebook. Then write the sentence three more times, this time using hyphens to divide the syllables of your two **Practice Words** and the **Primary Word**. If you don't know where to divide the word, look in the dictionary. Remember to underline the **Error-Causers** as you write them. Read the sentences out loud as you write them, emphasizing the **Error-Causer**.

Example A, Stage Three:

9.   touch, double, trouble

10.   If you touch the fire, you'll be in double trouble.
        If you touch the fire, you'll be in double trouble.
        If you touch the fire, you'll be in double trouble.

11.   If you touch the fire, you'll be in dou-ble trou-ble.
        If you touch the fire, you'll be in dou-ble trou-ble.
        If you touch the fire, you'll be in dou-ble trou-ble.

Example B, Stage Three:

9.   imply, rely, fly

10.   I did not imply that you rely on flying.
        I did not imply that you rely on flying.
        I did not imply that you rely on flying.

11.   I did not im-ply that you re-ly on fly-ing.
        I did not im-ply that you re-ly on fly-ing.
        I did not im-ply that you re-ly on fly-ing.

Desperate Measures

If you're reading this page, chances are you ran into trouble somewhere around **Step 6** or **Step 7**. Don't worry about it – you're in good hands! A lot of words in the English language are so unique that 1) they don't quite fit into any particular Word Lists, or 2) there aren't any other words that resemble their Error-Causer. Before we start talking about what to do with words that fit into those two categories, let's set those of you who don't really belong on the "Desperate Measures" page back to **Steps 6** and **7**.

If your problem is that your dictionary contains more than one phonetic pronunciation of your Primary Word, look up both of them in the manual. If you can only find one of them, that's great! Go back to **Step 6** and enter it into your notebook!

If you find two different Word Lists that seem to fit your Error Causer, then pick the one that makes the most sense to you. Sometimes your Primary Word will **rhyme** with one of the words in the Sub-Lists. If it doesn't, then it doesn't matter which one you pick.

If your Primary Word is so unique that it's Word List is only one or two words long, then you should do the **Rhyme, Rhyme, NOT QUITE Rhyme** exercise found in the **Additional Exercise** section **on page 12**. The **Rhyme, Rhyme, NOT QUITE Rhyme** exercise is powerful, and will help you spell words that prove troublesome. The same is true of the **Alternate Sound Match** exercise.

Those of you who are still here must have an extremely difficult word to spell. Just follow **Step 12** and you'll soon be back on track...

---

12. If the word you misspelled is so unique that you can't locate a Word List for it, you must construct a Solution Sentence. Directions are listed in the three steps below. After you construct the Solution Sentence, skip directly to **Step 10**, which you should do **twice** in your notebook.

   To create a Solution Sentence you should write a sentence in which...

   a.   the first word of the sentence begins with the first letter of the Error-Causer...

   b.   the second word in the sentence begins with the second letter of the Error-Causer, and...

   c.   the third word in the sentence begins with the third letter of the Error-Causer, if there is one. The last word in the sentence should be the word that you misspelled in the first place. There's an example on the next page.

Step 12 Example: co<u>lo</u>nel

<u>O</u>livia <u>l</u>oves colonels. (*Solution Sentence*, to take the
place of the *Primary Sentence* in **Step 10.**)

Additional Exercises

All of the **Additional Exercises** are designed to be used in conjunction with the **Primary Exercise**. Because different people learn in different ways, certain **Additional Exercises** will work more effectively for different students. It is suggested that you test the various exercises in order to determine which ones work best for your situation. All exercises should be practiced in the student's notebook whenever possible.

Rhyme, Rhyme, NOT QUITE Rhyme

Identify another Word List that contains your **Error-Causer**. Within it, choose two words that are both spelled and pronounced the same, thereby creating a rhyme. These will become your **Practice Words**. Write the two rhyming words next to one another, followed by the words *NOT QUITE* in capital letters, and then your **Primary Word**. Repeat three times. Then divide the three words according to their syllables (remember to look in the dictionary), and write them three more times. This exercise can be practiced on the **Primary Exercise** worksheet.

Example: *chief, thief, NOT QUITE science*
            chief, thief, NOT QUITE science...

Alternate Sound Match

Identify two separate Word Lists that contain your **Error-Causer**. The Error Causer will be the same, but it will be pronounced differently. Look through the two Word Lists and identify two words that contain your **Error-Causer** and are extremely easy to spell. These will be your **Practice Words**. Then write a sentence containing your two **Practice Words** and your **Primary Word**, underlining the **Error-Causer** each time it appears. The sentence should be written three times, and then three more times with the words' syllables divided with a hyphen. This exercise can be practiced on the **Primary Exercise** worksheet.

Example: *The chief's friends caused mischief*
            The chief's friends caused mischief...

Draw a Picture

Draw a picture (this works particularly well for young children) that depicts your **Primary Sentence**. Somewhere in the picture the **Primary Sentence** should be written.

Story Focus

Write a short story of no more than a page long using the three words contained in your **Primary Sentence** as many times as possible. Each time one of the three words is used, the letter or letter sound should be underlined.

Word Search

A parent or another student should fill one side of a piece of paper with 1) various misspellings of the word that was originally spelled wrong, and 2) many correct versions of the word as well. The student should be given a correct copy of the properly spelled word, and then told to cross out all the misspellings on the paper, and circle the correct ones.

Story Hodgepodge

After the student has completed a significant amount of **Primary Exercises**, try combining them all into a silly story.

Word String

A parent or another student should use a word processor to list a long string of letters with no spaces between them in which a **Primary Word** is repeated many times. The student's job is to go through the string and highlight or circle the word.

Article Exercise

Using an article from a newspaper or a magazine, highlight or circle the individual letters that spell your **Primary Word** and your **Practice Words**. For example, if your **Primary Word** was *friend* and your **Practice Words** were *chief* and *thief*, you should locate the first *f* in the article, and then look for the next *r*, followed by the rest of the letters in *friend*. Then, look for a *c* in order to spell the word *chief*, and eventually a *t* to spell the word *thief*. Ultimately, the article should be long enough to spell the three words several times.

Flash Cards

Create flash cards. On one side write your **Primary Word**, and on the other side write your **Primary Sentence**. Have someone show you the **Primary Word**, and read you the **Primary Sentence**, and then spell the two **Practice Words** within it.

Primary Exercise Sheet

Step One:

In the first box, write down your **Primary Word**. In the second box write down your **Error-Causer** followed by your **Phonetic Pattern**.

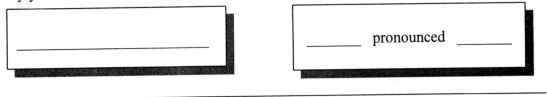

Step Two:

In the two boxes below, write your two **Practice Words**. Be sure to underline the **Error-Causer** in each.

Step Three:

Create a **Primary Sentence** using all three words, or practice the *Rhyme, Rhyme, NOT QUITE Rhyme* or *Alternate Sound Match* exercise below. Then practice the same exercise in your notebook.

Notebook Template

Stage One:

1. **My Original Sentence,** with the misspelled word circled:

2. **My Primary Word:**

3. **My Error Causer:**

4. **My Phonetic Pattern:**

5. **My Word List Phrase:** /___/ pronounced /___/ **or** silent /___/

6. **My Word List:**

7. **My Sub-List:**

Stage Two:

8, 8A, or 8B. My two **Practice Words** with the **Error-Causer** circled or underlined:

Stage Three:

9.   My **Primary Word**, followed by my two **Practice Words**:

10.   My **Primary Sentence**, written three times, with my **Error-Causers** underlined:

11. My **Primary Sentence**, written three times, with the syllables of the **Primary Word** and my two **Practice Words** divided, and my **Error-Causers** underlined:

Word Lists
A-1 through Z-3,
and their corresponding
Sub-Lists

Some Quick Reminders:

1. All Word Lists pertaining to the phonetic symbol /ə/ are labeled with the heading "Schwa Sound" so that they may be easily identified.

2. Because of its unique nature, all /ə/ sounds appear towards the end of their corresponding Word Lists, immediately before the "silent" letters.

3. Because the phonetic symbol /ə/ can be pronounced many, many different ways, you should look through ALL the schwa sounds within a given letter category before settling on one. It is therefore helpful to compare your **Primary Word** with the samples provided in each list. Simply read your **Primary Word** aloud, followed by the samples, and see which list provides the best match.

4. All "silent" letters may be found at the ends of their corresponding Word Lists.

5. Many of the Word Lists are categorized on the basis of whether or not their words contain silent /e/ endings. Therefore, be sure to look through several Word Lists before choosing one for use in a **Primary Exercise**.

6. Most of the Word Lists are based on vowels (/a/, /e/, /i/, /o/, /u/, and sometimes /y/), so if an **Error Causer** contains a vowel, be sure to look under the Word List for the vowel. If /tion/ is your **Error Causer**, for example, you should look for /t/ Word Lists *and* the /ion/ Word List as well.

List A-1

(/a/ pronounced /ā/ with no silent /e/ ending)
The sound /a/ as spelled and pronounced in the words

"crazy" and "haven"

ab	Abel
ac	aching, lacing, pacing, racing
ad	fading, stadium, waded, wading
ae	**See Lists A-11**
af	chafing, wafer
ag	caging, paging, raging, waging
ai	**See List A-14**
aj	Ajax
ak	baker, bakery, faker, maker
al	baling
am	tamer
an	caning
ao	aorta
ap	aping, stapling
as	basis, quasar, stasis
at	dated, dating, hated, hating, mated, mating, rated, rating, stated, stating
au	gauging
av	behaving, favor, favoring, haven, naval, navel, paving, raving, shaving, waving
ay	bay, day, gay, hay, lay, may, pay, ray, say, way
az	crazy, lazy

My Words...

_____   _____

_____   _____   _____

_____   _____   _____

_____   _____   _____

_____   _____   _____

_____   _____   _____

List A-2
(/a/ pronounced /ā/ with a silent /e/ ending)
The sound /a/ as spelled and pronounced in the words

"made" and "wage"

---

ab	able, babe, cable, fable, gable, table
ac	ace, ache, face, grace, lace, mace, pace, race,
ad	fade, jade, made, parade, trade, shade, wade
ae	Mae
af	safe
ag	age, cage, mage, page, plague, rage, sage, wage
ai	**See List A-15**
ak	bake, cake, fake, lake, make, rake, take, wake
al	ale, dale, gale, kale, male, pale, sale, vale
am	came, dame, fame, game, lame, name, same, tame
ap	ape, cape, gape, nape, tape
as	base, case, haste, paste, phase, taste, vase, waste
at	ate, crate, create, date, fate, gate, grate, hate, late, rate
av	behave, brave, cave, crave, gave, grave, shave
ay	**See List A-25**
az	craze, daze, gaze, haze, lazy, maze

My Words...

_____ _____

_____ _____ _____

_____ _____ _____

_____ _____ _____

_____ _____ _____

_____ _____ _____

_____ _____ _____

_____ _____ _____

List A-3
(/a/ pronounced /ā/)
The sound /a/ as spelled and pronounced in the words

"apple" and "aptitude"

---

ab	babble, crab, gab, jab, lab, slab, stab, tab, tablet
ac	active, actor, back, cackle, crack, fact, tack
ad	add, bad, back, fad, had, lad, mad, pad, , sad, tad
af	after, craft, draft, giraffe, graft, haft, raft, raffle
ag	bag, crag, dagger, hag, rag, sag, stag, tag, wag
al	album, balcony, falcon, fallow, gal, galley, pal, rally, reality, tally, valley, valid
am	**See List A-20**
an	**See List A-20**
ap	apple, cap, gap, happy, lap, map, nap, rap, sap
as	ask, chasm, crass, last, mast, nasty, pass, task
ash	ash, bash, cash, crash, dash, fashion, gash, hash, lash, mash, rash, sash
at	at, attic, bat, brat, cat, drat, hat, lattice, mat, pat, rat, ratify, sat, tattle, vat
au	laugh
av	avenue, average, avid, have
aw	**See List A-7**
ax	axiom, fax, lax, max, maximize, maximum, tax, wax
az	Aztec, azure, razz

My Words... _____ _____

_____ _____ _____

_____ _____ _____

_____ _____ _____

_____ _____ _____

_____ _____ _____

_____ _____ _____

_____ _____ _____

List A-4
(/a/ pronounced /ĕ/)
The sound /a/ as spelled and pronounced in the words

"any" and "many"

---

am   Thames
an   any, anything, many
ay   says

My Words...

    _____   _____   _____

_____   _____   _____

_____   _____   _____

_____   _____   _____

List A-5
(/a/ pronounced /ī/)
The sound /a/ as spelled and pronounced in the word

"aye"

---

ay   aye (meaning "yes")

My Words...

    _____   _____   _____

_____   _____   _____

_____   _____   _____

List A-6
(/a/ pronounced /ŏ/)
The sound /a/ as spelled and pronounced in the words

"swallow" and "wand"

al	swallow, wallow
an	wand, wander, want

My Words...

_____ _____

_____ _____ _____

_____ _____ _____

List A-7
(/a/ pronounced /ô/)
The sound /a/ as spelled and pronounced in the words

"autumn" and "water"

al	almost, altar, alter, although, halt, malt, salt, talk, walk
all	all, ball, call, fall, gall, hall, mall, pall, stall, wall
ar	**See List A-24**
at	water
au	August, autumn, cause, flaunt, Gaul, haughty, haul, haunt, jaunt, launch, laundry, maul, naughty, Paul, pause, taught, taunt, taut
aw	awe, awl, bawdy, caw, crawfish, draw, jaw, law, lawn maw, paw, raw, saw, yawn

My Words...

_____ _____

_____ _____ _____

_____ _____ _____

List A-8
(/a/ pronounced /ä/)
The sound /a/ as spelled and pronounced in the words

"calm" and "psalm"

---

ag   barrage, collage
al   alms, balm, calm, psalm
am   llama, samba
at   father
au   aunt, restaurant

My Words...

_____ _____ _____
_____ _____ _____
_____ _____ _____
_____ _____ _____

List A-9
(/aar/ pronounced /âr/)
The sound /a/ as spelled and pronounced in the word

"Aaron"

---

aa   Aaron

My Words...

_____ _____ _____
_____ _____ _____
_____ _____ _____

List A-10
(/aa/ pronounced /är/)
The sound /a/ as spelled and pronounced in the words

"aardvark" and "aardwolf"

---

aar   aardvark, aardwolf, bazaar

My Words...
_____ _____
_____ _____ _____
_____ _____ _____

List A-11
(/ae/ pronounced /ē/)
The sound /a/ as spelled and pronounced in the word

"Israel"

---

ael   Israel

My Words...
_____ _____
_____ _____ _____
_____ _____ _____

List A-12
(/aer/ pronounced /âr/)
The sound /a/ as spelled and pronounced in the words

"aerial" and "aerodynamic"

ae   aerial, aerobic, aerodynamic

My Words...

List A-13
(/agh/ pronounced /ē/)
The sound /a/ as spelled and pronounced in the word

"shillelagh"

agh   shillelagh

My Words...

List A-14
(/ai/ pronounced /ā/)
The sound /a/ as spelled and pronounced in the words

"hail" and "wait"

---

aid	aid, laid, maid, paid, raid
aif	waif
aig	straight
ail	avail, bail, fail, grail, hail, jail, mail, nail, pail, quail rail, sail, snail, tail, trail, wail
aim	aim, maim
ain	complain, gain, pain, plain, rain, saint, stain, sustain, train
ais	waist
ait	bait, gait, plait, wait, wraith
aiv	waive

My Words...

_____ _____ _____

_____ _____ _____

_____ _____ _____

_____ _____ _____

_____ _____ _____

_____ _____ _____

_____ _____ _____

_____ _____ _____

_____ _____ _____

_____ _____ _____

_____ _____ _____

List A-15
(/ai/ pronounced /ă/)
The sound /a/ as spelled and pronounced in the words

"daiquiri" and "plaid"

ai   daiquiri, plaid

My Words...

List A-16
(/ai/ pronounced /ĕ/)
The sound /a/ as spelled and pronounced in the word

"said"

aid   said
ain   again, against

My Words...

List A-17
(/ai/ pronounced /ī/)
The sound /a/ as spelled and pronounced in the words

"aisle" and "samurai"

---

ai   aisle, samurai

My Words...

List A-18
(/air/ pronounced /âr/)
The sound /a/ as spelled and pronounced in the words

"chair" and "hairy"

---

fair   fair, fairest, fairly, fairy
hair   chair, hair, hairiest, hairy
lair   lair
pair   pair

My Words...

List A-19
(/ăn/ followed by /g/, /k/, /qu/, or /x/)
The sound /a/ as spelled and pronounced in the words

"angle" and "bank"

ang	anger, sang, slang, tang
ank	bank, bankrupt
anqu	banquet
anx	anxiety, anxious

My Words...

_____ _____ _____

_____ _____ _____

_____ _____ _____

List A-20
(/ăm/ and /ăn/ which are never followed by /g/, /k/, /qu/, or /x/)
The sound /a/ as spelled in the words

"ample" and "cranberry"

am	ample, camera, damage, damp, famine, famished, hammer, jam, pamper, vampire
an	animal, brand, cranberry, dandy, fantasy, hand, land, pan, ran, sand, tan, van

My Words...

_____ _____ _____

_____ _____ _____

_____ _____ _____

_____ _____ _____

List A-21
(/aoh/ pronounced /ō/)
The letter /a/ as spelled and pronounced in the word

"pharaoh"

aoh   pharaoh

My Words... _____ _____

_____ _____ _____

List A-22
(/ar/ pronounced /är/)
The sound /a/ as spelled and pronounced in the words

"carbon" and "partner"

a	are, arm, army, art
bar	bar, barn,
car	car, carbon, card, art, carter, carve
dar	darn, dart
far	far, farm farthest, farther
gar	gar, garb, garden, gargle, garment
har	hard, hark, harm, harness, harp
jar	jar, ajar,
lar	alarm, lard
mar	martyr, smarmy, smart,
par	pardon, park, part, partner, party,
tar	retard, tar, target, tarnish, tarp
uar	jaguar
var	varmint, varnish
yar	yard, yarn

My Words... _____

_____ _____

_____ _____

_____ _____

_____ _____

_____ _____

_____ _____

_____ _____

List A-23
(/ar/ pronounced /âr/ with no silent /e/ ending)
The sound /a/ as spelled and pronounced in the words

"caramel" and "daring"

ara   caramel, caravan, marathon, parachute, paradise, paragraph, parakeet
are   area, Jared
ari   caribou, caring, daring, garish, garrison, marigold, mariner, snaring, staring
aro   baron, carousel, parody
arr   barrack, barracuda, barrier, carrion, marriage, narrow
ary   contrary, larynx, vary, wary

My Words...

military _____   _____

_____   _____   _____

_____   _____   _____

List A-24
(/ar/ pronounced /ôr/)
The sound /a/ as spelled and pronounced in the words

"quark" and "warranty"

ar   quarantine, quark, war, ward, warrant, warranty, warrior

My Words...

List A-25
(/are/ pronounced /âre/)
The sound /a/ as spelled and pronounced in the words

"care" and "dare"

bare	bare, barely
care	care, careful
dare	dare
fare	fare
hare	hare, share
mare	mare
nare	snare
rare	rare, rarely
tare	stare
ware	beware, ware

My Words...

List A-26
(/ay/ pronounced /ā/)
The sound /a/ as spelled and pronounced in the words

"decay" and "may"

bay	bay, baying
cay	cay, decay
day	day, today
gay	gay
hay	hay
jay	jay
lay	clay, lay
may	may
nay	nay
pay	pay
ray	gray, pray, ray, tray
say	say
way	sway, way

My Words...

List A-27
(Schwa Sound)
(/a/ pronounced /ə/)
The sound /a/ as spelled and pronounced in the words

"character" and "jubilant"

---

ac   character
ag   bandage, bondage, coverage, damage, village, wreckage
ah   hemorrhage
an   abundant, dominant, jubilant, militant, pleasant, relevant, tolerant valiant, vigilant
at   certificate, chocolate, considerate, desperate, temperate

My Words...

_____   _____   _____

_____   _____   _____

_____   _____   _____

_____   _____   _____

_____   _____   _____

_____   _____   _____

_____   _____   _____

_____   _____   _____

_____   _____   _____

_____   _____   _____

_____   _____   _____

List A-28
(Schwa Sound)
(/a/ pronounced /ə/)
The sound /a/ as spelled and pronounced in the words

"about" and "lapel"

---

a	aqua, Bosnia, insomnia, nostalgia, samba,
ab	about, abbreviate, abrupt, absurd, abundant, caboose, indispensable, irritable
ac	accost, account, acclaim, across
ach	machine
ad	adapt, addition, address, adept, adorn, adroit
af	affair, affiliate, afire, aflame, afraid
ag	again, agenda, agility, agree, aggressive
ah	ahead, ahoy, cheetah
aj	ajar
ak	akin
al	alarm, alack, along, aloof, calamity, malaria,
am	amaze, amend, ammonia, filament, predicament
an	anoint, announce, another, answer, banana, canary
ap	appear, approach, appropriate, lapel
aqu	aquatic
ar	arachnid, argue, arrange, caress, garage, harass
as	assail, assassin, assist
at	attack, attain, attend, attest, attract, attire
av	avail, avenge, avoid
aw	await, awake, award, away
az	azalea

My Words...

arrived

35

List A-29
(Schwa Sound)
(/aa/ pronounced /ə/ which more or less sounds like a /ĭ/)
The sound /a/ as spelled and pronounced in the word

"Isaac"

aac   Issac

My Words... _____ _____

_____ _____ _____

_____ _____ _____

List A-30
(Schwa Sound)
(/ai/ pronounced /ə/ which more or less sounds like /ĕ/)
The sound /a/ as spelled and pronounced in the words

"again" and "said"

ag   again, against
ai   said

My Words... _____ _____

_____ _____ _____

_____ _____ _____

List A-31
(Schwa Sound)
(/ai/ pronounced /ə/ which more or less sounds like /ĭ/)
The sound /a/ as spelled and pronounced in the words

"Britain" and "captain"

---

ain   bargain, Britain, captain fountain, mountain
ait   portrait

My Words... _____ _____

_____ _____ _____

_____ _____ _____

List A-32
(Schwa Sound)
(/al/ pronounced /əl/)
The sound /a/ as spelled and pronounced in the words

"moral" and "spinal"

---

al   botanical, final, magical, lyrical, hymnal, spinal, emerald, mineral, natural, rehearsal, tyrannical, metal, rental

My Words... _____ _____

_____ _____ _____

_____ _____ _____

List A-33
(Schwa Sound)
(/ar/ pronounced /ər/)
The sound /ar/ as spelled and pronounced in the words

"calendar" and "beggar"

---

ar   altar, awkward, beggar, blizzard, burglar, calendar, cellar, dollar, sugar

My Words...

_____   _____

_____   _____   _____

_____   _____   _____

_____   _____   _____

List B-1
(/b/ pronounced /b/)

---

ba   bad, baffle, bag, ball, ban, bar, bat, bawl
be   bed, bee, beef, beg, bell, best, bet
bi   bib, bid, big, bill, bin, bird, bit
bl   blab, black, bless, blind, block, blood, blow, blue, blur
bo   bob, body, bog, bond, bop, bored, boss, bottle
br   brag, brat, bravo, brawl, bring, broom
bu   bud, bug, bull, bump, bun, burr, bus, but
by   byline, bypass, bystander

My Words...

_____   _____

_____   _____   _____

_____   _____   _____

_____   _____   _____

List B-2
(/bb/ pronounced /b/)

---

bba   cabbage, cribbage
bbe   abbey, grabbed
bbi   bobbing, fibbing, mobbing, rabbit, robbing, stabbing
bbo   gibbon
bbl   babble, dribble, cobble, gobble, hobble, nibble, wobble
bby   Bobby, hobby, lobby, knobby, scrubby

My Words...

List B-3
(silent /b/)

---

bt   debt, doubt, subtle

My Words...

List C-1
(/c/ pronounced /ch/)

c   cello

My Words...

_____   _____

_____   _____   _____

_____   _____   _____

_____   _____   _____

List C-2
(/c/ pronounced /k/)

ca	cab, calf, camera, can, cap, car, cast, cat
cl	clan, clap, class, clay, clean, cleft, clerk, clip, clock, clod, clog, clop
co	cob, cod, con, cop, core, corn, cost, cot, cover
cr	crab, crack, creed, crew, crib, crop
cu	cub, cud, cuff, cup, cur, cuss, cut

My Words...

List C-3
(/c/ pronounced /s/)

ce   census, center, cedar, cell, dice, face, grace, ice, mice, pace, race, rice
ci   cider, cinder, citizen, citrus, civil
cy   cylinder, cypress, fancy, lacy, saucy

My Words...

_____   _____   _____

_____   _____   _____

_____   _____   _____

_____   _____   _____

_____   _____   _____

_____   _____   _____

List C-4
(/c/ pronounced /sh/)

ce   licorice
ci   ancient, conscious, musician, special

My Words...

_____   _____   _____

_____   _____   _____

_____   _____   _____

_____   _____   _____

List C-5
(/cc/ pronounced /k/)

cca	baccalaureate, baccarat, bacchanal, impeccable
cce	accept, accelerate, access, accident, soccer, success
cch	zucchini
cco	accord, account, accost, broccoli, stucco, tobacco
ccu	accumulate, accurate, accuse, accustom, hiccup, occur, succumb

My Words...

_____   _____

_____   _____   _____

_____   _____   _____

_____   _____   _____

List C-6
(/ch/)

cha	chalk, chamber, change, chapter, channel, charcoal, chase
che	cheap, check, cheek, cheese, cherry, chess, chest, chew
chi	chief, child, chill, chimney, chip, chipmunk, chisel
cho	choke, choose, chop
chu	chuck, chuckle, chug, chunk, churn
chy	grouchy, touchy

My Words...

_____   _____

_____   _____   _____

_____   _____   _____

_____   _____   _____

List C-7
(/ch/ pronounced /k/)

ch	Bach, loch, monarch
cha	chamomile, chaos, character, charisma, chasm
che	chemistry, lichen, orchestra, scheme
chi	aching, Chianti, chiropractor
chn	technical, technique
cho	chlorine, choir, chord, echo, school
chr	Christian, chrome, chronic
chy	anarchy, hierarchy

My Words...

List C-8
(/ch/ pronounced /sh/)

cha	chandelier, chagrin, chauffer, chauvinist
che	chef, chenille, moustache
chi	chivalry
chs	fuchsia
chu	chute, parachute

My Words...

List C-9
(/ck/ pronounced /k/)

---

ack	back, hack, lack, pack, rack, sack
eck	deck, fleck, neck, peck, wreck
ock	clock, dock, flock, hockey, lock, rock
uck	buck, duck, luck, puck, snuck, stuck, tuck

My Words...

List C-10
(/cq/ pronounced /k/)

cqu   acquaint, acquiesce, acquire, acquit, lacquer

My Words...

_____   _____   _____

_____   _____   _____

_____   _____   _____

_____   _____   _____

_____   _____   _____

List C-11
(/cz/ pronounced /z/)

cz   czar

My Words...

_____   _____   _____

_____   _____   _____

_____   _____   _____

_____   _____   _____

List C-12
(/cz/ pronounced /ch/)

_____

cz   Czech

My Words...	_____	_____
_____	_____	_____
_____	_____	_____
_____	_____	_____

_____

List C-13
(silent /c/)

_____

ch   yacht
ci   scissors
ct   indict, scent, victuals
cy   scythe

My Words...	_____	_____
_____	_____	_____
_____	_____	_____
_____	_____	_____
_____	_____	_____

List D-1
(/d/ pronounced /d/)

da	dad, daft, dam, damp, dance, dawn, day
de	decay, deep, demon, dentist, deny, destiny, detect
di	did, dig, dill, dim, dinner, dip
do	doctor, dog, doll, door
dr	drab, drink, drip, drop, dry
du	dub, dud, dug, dull, dust

My Words...

_____ _____

_____ _____ _____

_____ _____ _____

List D-2
(/d/ pronounced /j/)

du	educate, gradual, graduate
tu	congratulate

My Words...

_____ _____

_____ _____ _____

_____ _____ _____

_____ _____ _____

_____ _____ _____

_____ _____ _____

List D-3
(/dd/ pronounced /d/)

dd	add, odd
dde	adder, addict, addition, studded
ddh	Buddhism
ddi	giddiness, oddity
ddl	cuddly, doodle, noodle, middle, saddle, swaddle
ddo	haddock, paddock
ddr	address
ddy	daddy, muddy, toddy

My Words...

_____ _____ _____

_____ _____ _____

_____ _____ _____

_____ _____ _____

_____ _____ _____

List D-4
(silent /d/)

ed	Wednesday
nd	handkerchief, handsome

My Words...

_____ _____ _____

_____ _____ _____

_____ _____ _____

List E-1

(/ē/ with no silent /e/ ending)
The sound /e/ as spelled and pronounced in the words

"eject" and "legal"

---

e	be, behold, between, he, machete, reconsider, she, we
ea	**See List E-10**
eb	bebop, debar, Hebrew, Thebes, zebra
ec	decal, decent, declaw, decrypt, recap, recent, recover, secret
ed	cedar, media, median, mediate, medium, tedious
ee	preempt, reentry **(See Also List E-17)**
ef	defect (noun), refill, reflex, refund
eg	egret, legal, legion, regal, regent, region
eh	vehement
el	Helios
em	demon, demystify, femur, hemoglobin, lemur, rematch
en	genealogy, genial, genius, menial, penal, scene, Venus, venial
eo	**See List E-27**
eq	equal
er	cereal, serious, serum
et	detail, fetus, meteor, Peter, rethink
ev	evil, fever, revamp
ew	rework
ey	**See List E-39**

My Words... _____ _____

_____ _____ _____

_____ _____ _____

_____ _____ _____

_____ _____ _____

_____ _____ _____

_____ _____ _____

List E-2
(/ē/ with a silent /e/ ending)
The sound /e/ as spelled and pronounced in the words

"here" and "theme"

---

eb   debase, debate, rebate
ede   concede
eh   dehydrate, rehabilitate
el   feline
em   female, theme
ene   scene, serene
ere   here, severe
ete   discrete, Pete
ew   rewire, rewrite

My Words...

List E-3
(/e/ pronounced /ĕ/)
The sound /e/ as spelled and pronounced in the words

"hen" and "desperate"

ea	**See List E-12**
eb	debt, ebb, February, nebulous, rebel (noun)
ec	inspect, lecture, nectar, pectin, wreck
ed	bed, dread, fed, led, medical, red, Ted, wedding
ef	cleft, deft, heft, left
eg	beg, dreg, egg, leg, peg, regular
ei	**See List E-21**
ek	dekagram
el	bell, citadel, dell, fell, gelding, hell, knelt, melt, pelt, quell, relish, sell, tell, welt
em	demographics, empty, gem, hem, hemp, lemon, memory, nemesis, temporary
en	den, defend, dent, fender, hen, lend, men, pen, pendant, render, send
eo	**See List E-26**
ep	hepatitis, inept, intercept, leprosy, pepper, repetition, tepid
equ	equity, requiem
er	**See List E-29**
es	attest, best, chest, dress, fester, festival, less, mess, nest, pest, quest, west, zest
et	bet, fetter, get, letter, metro, net
eu	**See List E-34**
ev	bevel, clever, ever, forever, level, never, revelry, sever
ex	hex, hexagon, lexicon, Mexico, nexus, Texas, vex

My Words...

endzone

List E-4
(/e/ pronounced /ā/)
The sound /e/ as spelled and pronounced in the word

"deity" and "ballet"

e   café
ei   deity
et   ballet, claret, valet
ev   rendezvous

My Words... _____ _____

_____ _____ _____

_____ _____ _____

List E-5
(/e/ pronounced /är/)
The sound /e/ as spelled and pronounced in the word

"sergeant"

ea   **See List E-9**
er   sergeant

My Words... _____ _____

_____ _____ _____

_____ _____ _____

List E-6
(/e/ pronounced /ĭ/)
The sound /e/ as spelled and pronounced in the words

"stranded" and "handed"

---

en	England, English
ded	branded, defended, handed, stranded
een	**See List E-18**
ket	blanket, bucket, market, trinket, wicked
let	owlet, pallet, wallet
quet	banquet
res	forest
ret	pretty
ted	antiquated, blanketed, quieted, related, stated

My Words... _____ _____

_____ _____ _____

_____ _____ _____

List E-7
(/e/ pronounced /ŏ/)
The sound /e/ as spelled and pronounced in the words

"encore" and "entrée"

---

ea	**See List E-15**
en	encore, entrée

My Words... _____ _____

_____ _____ _____

List E-8
(/ea/ pronounced /âr/)
The sound /e/ as spelled and pronounced in the words

"pear" and "wear"

ear   bear, pear, swear, tear (as in *wear and tear*), wear

My Words...

List E-9
(/ea/ pronounced /är/)
The sound /e/ as spelled and pronounced in the word

"heart" and "hearth"

ear   heart, hearth

My Words...

List E-10
(/ea/ pronounced /ē/ with no silent /e/ ending)
The sound /e/ as spelled and pronounced in the words

"each" and "leaf"

---

ea	guinea, sea, tea
eac	each, beach, leach, peach, reach, teach
ead	bead, lead, mead, read
eaf	leaf
eak	beak, leak, peak, streak, weak
eal	deal, heal, meal, peal, real, seal, steal, veal, zeal
eam	beam, cream, dream, seam, steam
ean	bean, dean, lean, mean
eap	heap, leap, reap
ear	ear, fear, gear, hear, near, rear, tear (as in *teardrop*)
eas	ease, easy, easel, leash weasel
eat	eat, beat, feat, heat, meat, neat, seat, wheat
eath	beneath, bequeath, heath, sheath, wreath, underneath
eav	beaver
eau	beauty

My Words...

meat

neat

List E-11
(/ea/ pronounced /ē/ with a silent /e/ ending)
The sound /e/ as spelled and pronounced in the words

"league" and "weave"

eag   beagle, eagle, league
eas   ease,
eav   bereave, cleave, heave, leave, weave

My Words...   _____   _____

please   _____   _____

_____   _____   _____

List E-12
(/ea/ pronounced /ĕ/)
The sound /e/ as spelled and pronounced in the words

"endeavor" and "weapon"

ea   endeavor, weapon

My Words...   _____   _____

_____   _____   _____

_____   _____   _____

_____   _____   _____

List E-13
(/ear/ pronounced /ûr/)
The sound /e/ as spelled and pronounced in the words

"earnest" and "learn"

---

ear   earn, earnest, earth, heard, learn

My Words...

heard

heart

List E-14
(/eau/ pronounced /ō/)
The sound /e/ as spelled and pronounced in the word

"bureau"

---

eau   bureau

My Words...

List E-15
(/eau/ pronounced /ŏ/)
The sound /e/ as spelled and pronounced in the word

"bureaucracy"

eauc   bureaucracy

My Words... _____   _____

_____   _____   _____

List E-16
(/ed/ in which the /e/ is silent)
The sound /e/ as spelled and pronounced in the words

"embarrassed" and "equipped"

bed	bobbed, clubbed, grabbed
ced	diced, sliced
ged	bagged, bogged, clogged
hed	coughed, ploughed
ied	lied, pitied, tied, taxied
ked	backed, clocked, cracked
led	appalled, balled, called, mailed
med	crammed, drummed, jammed
ned	craned, drained, learned, tanned
ped	bopped, cropped, draped
red	dared, fired, flared, glared
sed	crossed, dressed, passed, tossed
ued	glued, hued, sued
ved	loved, moved, raved, saved, waved
wed	clawed, pawed, rowed, sawed
xed	boxed, taxed, vexed, waxed
yed	dyed, hayed, vied
zed	crazed, dazed, fizzed, gazed, razzed

My Words...

_____   _____

_____   _____

_____   _____

_____   _____

_____   _____

_____   _____

List E-17
(/ee/ pronounced /ē/)
The sound /e/ as spelled and pronounced in the words

"bee" and "seed"

---

ee	bee, fee, knee, see
eec	beech, breech, leech
eed	deed, creed, exceed, feed, heed, need, proceed, seed, succeed, weed
eef	beef, reef,
eek	cheek, geek, leek, meek, reek, week
eel	eel, feel, heel, kneel, peel, reel, steel, wheel
eem	deem, seem
een	between, seen
eep	beep, creep, deep, peep, sleep, steep, steeple, weep
eer	beer, deer, leer, peer, queer, seer, sheer, steer, veer
ees	bees, fees, knees,
eet	beet, feet, meet
eeth	teeth
eev	peeve
eez	breeze, freeze, sneeze

My Words...

keeping

List E-18
(/ee/ pronounced /ĭ/)
The sound /e/ as spelled and pronounced in the word

"been"

een   been

My Words...

_____   _____   _____

_____   _____   _____

_____   _____   _____

_____   _____   _____

List E-19
(/ei/ pronounced /ā/)
The sound /e/ as spelled and pronounced in the word

"beige"

ei   beige, heir

My Words...

_____   _____   _____

_____   _____   _____

_____   _____   _____

_____   _____   _____

List E-20
(/ei/ pronounced /ē/)
The sound /e/ as spelled and pronounced in the words

"conceive" and "receipt"

---

eip   receipt
eis   leisure
eit   conceit, either
eiv   conceive, receive
eiz   seize

My Words...

_____   _____

_____   _____   _____

_____   _____   _____

_____   _____   _____

List E-21
(/ei/ pronounced /ĕ/)
The sound /e/ as spelled and pronounced in the word

"heifer"

---

eif   heifer

My Words...

_____   _____

_____   _____   _____

_____   _____   _____

List E-22
(/ei/ pronounced /ĭ/)
The sound /e/ as spelled and pronounced in the words

"height" and "sleight"

eigh   height, sleight
eign   feign, reign
ein   reindeer, skein, vein

My Words...

List E-23
(/ei/ pronounced /ĭ/)
The sound /e/ as spelled and pronounced in the word

"forfeit" and "surfeit"

eig   foreign, sovereign
eit   forfeit, surfeit

My Words...

List E-24
(/eigh/ pronounced /ā/)
The sound /e/ as spelled and pronounced in the words

"eight" and "weight"

---

eigh   sleigh
eighb   neighbor
eign   feign, reign
eight   eight, weight

My Words...	_____	_____
_____	_____	_____
_____	_____	_____

List E-25
(/en/ in which the /e/ is silent)
The sound /e/ as spelled and pronounced in the words

"garden" and "harden"

---

en   garden, harden, marten

My Words...	_____	_____
_____	_____	_____
_____	_____	_____
_____	_____	_____
_____	_____	_____

List E-26
(/eo/ pronounced /ĕ/)
The sound /e/ as spelled and pronounced in the words

"Geoffrey" and "jeopardy"

eof   Geoffrey
eop   jeopardy, leopard

My Words...

List E-27
(/eo/ pronounced /ē/)
The sound /e/ as spelled and pronounced in the words

"people" and "theory"

eop   people
eor   theory

My Words...

List E-28
(/eo/ pronounced /ō/)
The sound /e/ as spelled and pronounced in the word

"yeoman"

eo   yeoman

My Words...

       _____   _____

_____   _____   _____

_____   _____   _____

List E-29
(/er/ pronounced /ĕr/)
The sound /e/ as spelled and pronounced in the words

"America" and "cherry"

er   America, monastery
err   berry, cherry, terror

My Words...

       _____   _____

_____   _____   _____

_____   _____   _____

_____   _____   _____

List E-30
(/er/ pronounced /ûr/)
The sound /e/ as spelled and pronounced in the words

"herd" and "vertical"

er   clerk, fiery, her, herb, herd, nerve, serve, vertical

My Words...

quarter

List E-31
(/ere/ pronounced /âr/)
The sound /e/ as spelled and pronounced in the words

"there" and "where"

ere   there, where

My Words...

List E-32
(/eu/ pronounced /o͞o/)
The sound /e/ as spelled and pronounced in the words

"connoisseur" and "maneuver"

eur   connoisseur
eum   rheumatism
euv   maneuver

My Words...

List E-33
(/eu/ pronounced /yo͞o/)
The sound /e/ as spelled and pronounced in the word

"feud"

eud   feud

My Words...

List E-34
(/eur/ pronounced /ĕr/)
The sound /e/ as spelled and pronounced in the word

"chauffeur"

eur   chauffeur

My Words...

List E-35
(/ew/ pronounced /ō/)
The sound /e/ as spelled and pronounced in the word

"sew"

ew   sew

My Words...

List E-36
(/ew/ pronounced /o͞o/)
The sound /e/ as spelled and pronounced in the words

"new" and "threw"

ew   dew, few, flew, lewd, new, shrew, strewn, threw

My Words...

_____   _____

_____   _____   _____

_____   _____   _____

_____   _____   _____

List E-37
(/ew/ pronounced /yo͞o/)
The sound /e/ as spelled and pronounced in the word

"pewter" and "skewer"

kew   skewer
pew   pewter

My Words...

_____   _____

_____   _____   _____

_____   _____   _____

_____   _____   _____

List E-38
(/ey/ pronounced /ā/)
The sound /e/ as spelled and pronounced in the words

"they" and "whey"

ey   hey, prey, survey, they, whey

My Words...	_____	_____
_____	_____	_____
_____	_____	_____

List E-39
(/ey/ pronounced /ē/)
The sound /e/ as spelled and pronounced in the words

"honey" and "key"

key   donkey, key, monkey
ley   holey
ney   attorney, chimney, honey, money
oey   gooey, phooey
sey   curtsy

My Words...	_____	_____
_____	_____	_____
_____	_____	_____
_____	_____	_____

List E-40
(/ey/ pronounced /ī/)
The sound /e/ as spelled and pronounced in the word

"eye"

ey   eye, geyser

My Words...

List E-41
(Schwa Sound)
(/e/ pronounced /ə/)
The sound /e/ as spelled and pronounced in the words

"benefit" and "category"

ea	**See List E-42**
eb	Caleb
ec	necessitate
ef	benefit
eg	category, delegate
ei	reveille
el	**See List E-43**
em	complement, demand, system
en	**See List E-44**
eo	**See List E-45**
ep	deploy, elephant
er	**See List E-46**
es	earnest **(See Also List E-47)**
et	kilometer, thermometer

My Words...

List E-42
(Schwa Sound)
(/ea/ pronounced /ə/ which more or less sounds like /ĭ/)
The letter /e/ as spelled and pronounced in the words

"damageable" and "pageant"

eab   damageable, manageable, noticeable
ean   pageant, vengeance

My Words...

_____ _____

_____ _____ _____

_____ _____ _____

List E-43
(Schwa Sound)
(/el/ pronounced "əl")
The letter /e/ as spelled and pronounced in the words

"fuel" and "jewel"

bel	Babel, label
gel	bagel
hel	bachelor
mel	camel
nel	panel
uel	fuel
vel	envelope, reveille, travel
wel	jewel

My Words...

_____ _____

_____ _____

_____ _____

_____ _____

_____ _____

List E-44
(Schwa Sound)
(/en/ pronounced /ən/)
The letter /e/ as spelled and pronounced in the words

"children" and "moment"

den   dependent, different
gen   emergency
ken   hearken
men   moment, pavement women
nen   linen
pen   happen, sharpen
ren   children
sen   arsenal
ven   covenant, heaven, leaven

My Words...

List E-45
(Schwa Sound)
(/eo/ pronounced /əo/)
The letter /e/ as spelled and pronounced in the words

"bludgeon" and "dungeon"

---

ceous   herbaceous
geon   bludgeon, dungeon
geous   courageous
heon   luncheon, truncheon
teous   righteous

My Words...

List E-46
(Schwa Sound)
(/er/ pronounced /ər/)
The letter /e/ as spelled and pronounced in the words

"passenger" and "hamper"

---

ber	clamber
der	dander, finder, grinder, modern, slander
fer	puffer, stiffer, stuffer
ger	passenger, singer
her	brother, mother, other
ker	bicker, hacker, slacker, ticker
ler	doodler, handler
mer	hammer, stammer
ner	banner, dinner, gunner, miner, runner
per	hamper, operate, pamper, proper
ser	adviser
ter	lantern, literal, litter
ver	clover, cover, giver, liver

My Words...

_____ _____ _____

_____ _____ _____

_____ _____ _____

_____ _____ _____

_____ _____ _____

_____ _____ _____

_____ _____ _____

_____ _____ _____

_____ _____ _____

List E-47
(Schwa Sound)
(/es/ pronounced /əs/)
The letter /e/ as spelled and pronounced in the words

"fixes" and "watches"

ches   catches, matches, patches, watches
shes   dishes, fishes, wishes
ses   hisses, losses, misses, mosses
xes   boxes, fixes, foxes
zes   fizzes, frizzes

My Words...
_____   _____

_____   _____   _____

_____   _____   _____

_____   _____   _____

List E-48
(silent /e/ which creates an /ē/ sound in the letter /i/)
The letter /e/ as spelled and pronounced in the words

"machine" and "routine"

ine   machine, routine

My Words...
_____   _____

_____   _____   _____

_____   _____   _____

List E-49

(silent /e/)
The letter /e/ as spelled and pronounced in the words

"care" and "trace"

---

be	babe, cube, robe, tribe, vibe
ce	dice, entice, face, grace, lace
de	made, mode, nude, ride, rude
fe	fife, life, wife
ge	cage, huge, page, rage, sage, wage
ie	die, fire, lie, pie, tie, vie
ke	bake, cake, fake, hike, like, wake
me	crime, dime, dome, grime, home
ne	alone, bone, cone, fine, pine, tune
oe	doe, foe, hoe, potatoes, toe, woe
pe	cape, drape, grope, hope, pipe, ripe, wipe
re	bore, core, cure, dire, hire, rare, sire, tire
se	abuse, base, case, dose, fuse, hose, nose
te	ate, bite, cute, date, gate, kite, rate, rite
ve	behave, clove, dive, dove, gave, wave
we	owe

My Words...

_____   _____   _____

_____   _____   _____

_____   _____   _____

_____   _____   _____

_____   _____   _____

_____   _____   _____

_____   _____   _____

_____   _____   _____

_____   _____   _____

List E-50

(silent /e/)

The letter /e/ as spelled and pronounced in the words

"edge" and "favorite"

---

ce	abundance, adequate, entrance, importance, justice, voice
fe	carafe, giraffe
ge	badge, bridge, collage, college, edge, foliage, garage, ledge, postage, singe, wedge
he	loathe
le	bundle, candle, horrible, juggle, mumble, rubble, rumble, tumble, stumble, terrible
me	awesome, become, come, some, someone
ne	done, engine, gone, medicine, one
pe	Europe
que	burlesque, grotesque
re	are, ensure, failure, macabre, measure, seizure, were
se	choose, defense, dense, eclipse, immense, lose, purchase, whose
te	brunette, chocolate, favorite, fortunate, infinite, minute, opposite
ve	combative, competitive, comprehensive, deserve, executive, give, swerve
we	awe, awesome

My Words...

_____ _____ _____

_____ _____ _____

_____ _____ _____

_____ _____ _____

_____ _____ _____

_____ _____ _____

_____ _____ _____

_____ _____ _____

_____ _____ _____

_____ _____ _____

List F-1
(/f/ pronounced /f/)

fa	fact, fad, fall, fan, fast, fat, fawn
fe	fed, fell, fen, fester, fetch
fi	fib, fig, fill, film, fin, fist, fit, fizz
fl	flag, flat, flip, flop, Florida, fly
fo	fog, foot, fop, for, fork
fr	Frank, free, frog, from, frost, fry
fu	full, fun, fur, fuzz

My Words...

_____   _____   _____

_____   _____   _____

_____   _____   _____

_____   _____   _____

_____   _____   _____

List F-2
(/f/ pronounced /v/)

of   of

My Words...

_____   _____   _____

_____   _____   _____

_____   _____   _____

List F-3
(/ff/ pronounced /f/)

ff	buff, chaff, scruff, staff, whiff
ffa	affair, affect, affirm, afford, staffing
ffe	coffer, offense, offer, suffer
ffi	coffin, effigy, office, puffin, sniffing, sufficient
ffs	offspring, offstage
ffr	saffron
ffy	puffy, taffy
ffl	baffle, sniffle, waffle

My Words...

_____   _____   _____

_____   _____   _____

_____   _____   _____

_____   _____   _____

List G-1
(/g/ pronounced /g/)

ga	gab, gag, gall, gap, gas
ge	get
gi	gig, girl
gl	glad, glass
go	go, gob, God, golly, got, govern
gr	grab, green, grow
gu	gull, gum, gun, guppy, Gus, gut

My Words...

_____   _____   _____

_____   _____   _____

_____   _____   _____

_____   _____   _____

List G-2
(/gg/ pronounced /g/)

---

gga   baggage, beggar, haggard, toboggan
gge   bagged, bigger, bogged, dagger, fogged, gagged, nugget, rigged
ggr   aggravate, aggressive, aggressor
ggy   baggy, boggy, foggy, soggy
ggl   giggle, googolplex, snuggle, struggle, toggle

My Words...

List G-3
(/g/ pronounced /j/)

---

ge   beige, bulge, college, generous, gentle, genre, prestige, refrigerator
gi   giant, regime

My Words...

List G-4
(/gh/ pronounced /g/)

gha   Ghana, ghastly
ghe   gherkin, ghetto, spaghetti
gho   ghost, ghoul
ghy   dinghy

My Words...

List G-5
(/gn/ pronounced /n/)

gna   gnarl, gnat, gnash, gnaw, gnome, gnu

My Words...

List G-6
(/gn/ pronounced /ny/)

---

gn   cognac, poignant

My Words...

_____   _____   _____

_____   _____   _____

_____   _____   _____

_____   _____   _____

List G-7
(/gh/ pronounced /f/)

---

gh   cough, enough, laugh, rough, tough

My Words...

_____   _____   _____

_____   _____   _____

_____   _____   _____

_____   _____   _____

List G-8
(silent /g/)

gh   dough, plough, though
ght   eight, distraught, drought, haughty, flight, naught, straight, taught, thought
gn   align, arraign, champagne, foreign, reign, sovereign
gm   diaphragm, phlegm

My Words...

List H-1
(/h/ pronounced /h/)

ha	had, hag, hall, ham, hand, hard, has, hat
he	he, hen, Henry, her
hi	hi, hid, hill, him, hip, his, hit
ho	hog, hop, hope, hot, holy
hu	hub, huff, hug, hull, hum, hut

My Words...

_____ _____ _____

_____ _____ _____

_____ _____ _____

_____ _____ _____

_____ _____ _____

List H-2
(silent /h/)

h	cheetah, messiah
ha	exhaust
he	heir, rhetoric, shepherd
ho	honest, hour

My Words...

_____ _____ _____

_____ _____ _____

_____ _____ _____

_____ _____ _____

List I-1

(/ī/ with no silent /e/)
The sound /i/ as spelled and pronounced in the words

"fiber" and "icon"

---

i	I, fungi, rabbi
ia	diabolical, diagram, diagonal, dial, diaper, giant, liar, Niagara, Siam, trial
ib	fiber, libel, vibration
ic	icon, microchip
id	idea, identical
ie	anxiety, client, diet fiery, pliers, quiet, shier, society (**Also See List I-14**)
if	bifocal
ig	align, digest, flight, high, Niger, tiger
ik	biking, hiking, Viking
il	bilateral, child, silo, wild
im	climb, lima bean
in	bind, diner, find, hind, pint, rind,
io	biology, lion, pioneer, pious, riot, violent
ip	biped, siphon, piping, ripen, stipend
ir	Iran, iron, pirate, siren, virus
is	bison, Christ, island
it	italic, item, mitosis, titan, titanic, vitamin
iv	ivory, ivy, saliva, rival
iw	biweekly

My Words...

_____   _____   _____

_____   _____   _____

_____   _____   _____

_____   _____   _____

_____   _____   _____

_____   _____   _____

_____   _____   _____

_____   _____   _____

List I-2
(/ĭ/ with a silent /e/ ending)
The sound /i/ as spelled and pronounced in the words

"wise" and "tries"

---

ib	hibernate, tribe, vibe
ic	bicycle, dice, ice, lice, mice, nice, rice
id	bide, confide, hide, ride, side
ie	**See List I-9**
if	fife, knife, life, rifle, trifle, wife
ig	oblige
ik	bike, hike, likable, like, pike
il	bile, file, mile, Nile, pile, rile, silence, tile
im	dime, lime, mime, time
in	dine, fine, line, mine, pine, vine, wine
ip	gripe, pipe, ripe
ir	dire, fire, hire, tire, wire
is	advise, rise, wise
it	bite, kite, rite, site, writhe
iv	dives, five, hive, jive, lives (*noun, plural of "life"*), wives
iz	capitalize, magnetize, prize, sizable, size

My Words...

_____ _____ _____

_____ _____ _____

_____ _____ _____

_____ _____ _____

_____ _____ _____

_____ _____ _____

_____ _____ _____

List I-3
(/ĭ/ with no silent /e/ ending)
The sound /i/ as spelled and pronounced in the words

"big" and "fill"

ia   **(Also See List I-8)**

ib   bib, crib, drip, fib, gibbet, giblets, gibbon, jib, lib, liberal, liberty, lick, lip, lipstick, nib, nibble, rib

ic   diction, dictionary, fiction, fictitious, picture, tic, victory

id   bid, flaccid, placid, did, candid, splendid, confident, hid, kid, lid, rid, Yiddish

if   biff, cliff, different, fifty, gift, if, jiffy, lift, nifty, rift, sift, tiff, whiff

ig   big, bigot, dig, fig, gig, jig, ligament, pig, rig, significance, significant, wig

il   bill, children, fill, gill, hill, ill, kill, militant, military, mill, million, pill, quill, sill,

im   crimp, dimple, him, imp, import, important, limb, limp, rim, shim,

in   bin, cabin, cinder, chin, din, dinner, fin, finish, gibbon, grin, in, indigo, inhabit, injury, instant, intelligent, jinx, mini, minimum, pin, resin, sin, tin, vinegar, win, zinnia

ip   blip, chip, clip, dip, drip, grip, hip, hipster, jip, lip, nip, pip, quip, rip, sip, tip, whip, zip

ir   irritate, spirit

is   blister, Christopher, crisis, dismiss, fish, hinder, isthmus, kiss, list, miss

it   bit, bandit, ditz, citizen, fit, gambit, hit, it, knit, lit, little, mitt, mitten, nit, nitpick, pit, quit, sit, whittle, wit, witness

iv   living, privilege, privy, vivify

iz   fizz

My Words...

_____ _____ _____

_____ _____ _____

_____ _____ _____

_____ _____ _____

_____ _____ _____

_____ _____ _____

_____ _____ _____

List I-4
(/ĭ/ with a silent /e/ ending)
The sound /ĭ/ as spelled and pronounced in the words

"porridge" and "vestige"

---

ibble	dribble, quibble
ice	crevice, office
idge	cartridge, porridge, ridge
iddle	middle, piddle, riddle
ige	vestige
ine	heroine
ite	opposite
ive	active, give, live

My Words...

List I-5

(/i/ pronounced /ē/)

The sound /i/ as spelled and pronounced in the words

"piano" and "broccoli"

I	Ian
bi	bistro
ci	appreciate, associate, conscientious, mediate
di	custodian, audience, guardian, handiwork, hardiness, idiot media, shadiness
fi	fiancé, fiord
ki	kiosk, riskiness, shakiness, ski
li	alien, broccoli, cauliflower, filial, liaison, liter, loneliness, ugliness
mi	bohemian, simian
ni	Palestinian
io	hilarious, radio
pi	happiness, piano, pilaf, piquant, pizza, utopia
ri	burrito, chariot, carrier, debris, industrial, patriot, satirical, scariness, warrior
si	easier, physiology
ti	petite, pitiful, plentiful
ui	mosquito
vi	abbreviate, alleviate, deviant
wi	kiwi

My Words...

_____   _____   _____

_____   _____   _____

_____   _____   _____

_____   _____   _____

_____   _____   _____

_____   _____   _____

_____   _____   _____

List I-6

(/i/ pronounced /ē/ with a silent /e/ ending)
The sound /i/ as spelled and pronounced in the words

"machine" and "vaccine"

ice	police
igue	fatigue
ine	machine, magazine, routine, vaccine
ique	technique

My Words...

_____   _____

_____   _____   _____

_____   _____   _____

List I-7

(/i/ pronounced /ûr/)
The sound /i/ as spelled and pronounced in the words

"first" and "flirt"

ir   bird, circle, circuit, circus, firm, first, flirt, girl, sir, stir, stirrup

My Words...

_____   _____

_____   _____   _____

_____   _____   _____

List I-8
(/iag/ pronounced /ǐ/)
The sound /i/ as spelled and pronounced in the word

"carriage"

---

iag   carriage, marriage

My Words... _____   _____

_____   _____   _____

_____   _____   _____

List I-9
(/ie/ pronounced /ē/ with no silent /e/ ending)
The sound /i/ as spelled and pronounced in the words

"belief" and "relief"

---

ie   movie
ied   buried, ferried, harried, married, tarried, worried
ief   chief, belief, thief, relief
iek   shriek
iel   field, shield, wield, yield
ien   fiend, lien
ier   cashier, tier
ies   candies, dummies, priest, puppies twenties

My Words... _____   _____

chief _____   _____   _____

_____   _____   _____

_____   _____   _____

List I-10
(/ie/ pronounced /ē/ with a silent /e/ ending)
The sound /i/ as spelled and pronounced in the words

"believe" and "relieve"

iece   niece, piece
iege   liege, siege
iene   hygiene
ieve   achieve, believe, receive, relieve
ieze   frieze

My Words...

_____   _____   _____

_____   _____   _____

_____   _____   _____

List I-11
(/ie/ pronounced /ĕ/)
The sound /i/ as spelled and pronounced in the word

"friend"

ie   friend

My Words...

_____   _____

_____   _____

_____   _____

List I-12
(/ie/ pronounced /ĭ/ with a silent /e/ ending)
The sound /ĭ/ as spelled and pronounced in the word

"sieve"

ie   sieve

My Words...
_____   _____
_____   _____   _____
_____   _____   _____
_____   _____   _____

List I-13
(/ie/ pronounced /ĭ/ with no silent /e/ ending)
The sound /ĭ/ as spelled and pronounced in the word

"mischief"

ief   mischief

My Words...
_____   _____
_____   _____   _____
_____   _____   _____

List I-14
(/ie/ pronounced /ī/)
The sound /i/ as spelled and pronounced in the words

"cried" and "dried"

ied   cried, dried, fried, tried
ien   science
ies   cries, dries, fries, tries

My Words...

Tried

List I-15
(/ier/ pronounced /îr/)
The sound /i/ as spelled and pronounced in the words

"cavalier" and "chandelier"

ier   cashier, cavalier, chandelier, pier

My Words...

List I-16
(/ieu/ pronounced /o͞o/)
The sound /i/ as spelled and pronounced in the word

"lieutenant"

ieut   lieutenant

My Words...

_____ _____ _____

_____ _____ _____

_____ _____ _____

_____ _____ _____

List I-17
(/iew/ pronounced /yo͞o/)
The sound /i/ as spelled and pronounced in the word

"view"

iew   view

My Words...

_____ _____ _____

_____ _____ _____

_____ _____ _____

List I-18
(/ig/ pronounced /ī/)
The sound /i/ as spelled and pronounced in the words

"sigh" and "light"

---

igh   high, nigh, sigh
ign   sign
ight   delight, fight, flight, light, might, night, plight, right, sight

My Words...   _____   _____

_____   _____   _____

_____   _____   _____

List I-19
(/ii/)
The sound /i/ as spelled (but *not necessarily pronounced*) in the words

"Hawaii" and "skiing"

---

aii   Hawaii
dii   radii
eii   Pompeii
kii   skiing
xii   taxiing

My Words...   _____   _____

_____   _____   _____

_____   _____   _____

(/ir/ pronounced /îr/)
The sound /i/ as spelled and pronounced in the word

"virulent"

iru   virulent

My Words... _____ _____

_____ _____ _____

List I-21
(Schwa Sound)
(/i/ pronounced /ə/)
The sound /i/ as spelled and pronounced in the words

"audible" and "legible"

iba	cannibal
ible	accessible, audible, credible, edible, irresistible, legible, responsible
id	residence
il	family, privilege
im	animal
in	continent, dominate, infinite
ine	determine, discipline, medicine
ip	participate
ite	definite, infinite

My Words... _____ _____

_____ _____ _____

_____ _____ _____

_____ _____ _____

(Schwa Sound)
(/ia/ pronounced /ə/)
The sound /i/ as spelled and pronounced in the words

"Asia" and "Russia"

---

sia   Asia, parliament, Prussia, Russia

My Words...

_____

_____

_____

List I-23
(Schwa Sound)
(/ial/ pronounced /əl/)
The sound "i" as spelled and pronounced in the words

"influential" and "martial"

---

cial   financial, social, substantial
ntial   influential
rtial   martial, partial

My Words...

_____

_____

_____

List I-24
(Schwa Sound)
(/ian/ pronounced /ən/)
The sound /i/ as spelled and pronounced in the words

"musician" and "physician"

---

ian   Christian, Egyptian, electrician, musician, Norwegian, patrician, physician

My Words...
_____   _____
_____   _____   _____
_____   _____   _____
_____   _____   _____

List I-25
(Schwa Sound)
(/ian/ pronounced /yən/)
The sound /i/ as spelled and pronounced in the words

"brilliant" and "Italian"

---

ian   brilliant, Italian

My Words...
_____   _____
_____   _____   _____
_____   _____   _____

List I-26
(Schwa Sound)
(/iar/ pronounced /ər/)
The sound /i/ as spelled and pronounced in the words

"familiar" and "similar"

---

iar   familiar, similar

My Words...

List I-27
(Schwa Sound)
(/iel/ pronounced /əl/)
The sound /i/ as spelled and pronounced in the words

"Daniel" and "spaniel"

---

iel   Daniel, spaniel

My Words...

List I-28
(Schwa Sound)
(/ien/ pronounced /ən/)
The sound /i/ as spelled and pronounced in the words

"ancient" and "patient"

ience   convenience, patience
cient   ancient
tient   convenient, patient

My Words...

_____   _____   _____

_____   _____   _____

_____   _____   _____

List I-29
(Schwa Sound)
(/ier/ pronounced /ər/)
The sound /i/ as spelled and pronounced in the word

"soldier"

dier   soldier

My Words...

_____   _____   _____

_____   _____   _____

_____   _____   _____

List I-30
(Schwa Sound)
(/il/ pronounced /əl/)
The sound /i/ as spelled and pronounced in the word

"fossil"

sil   fossil

My Words... _____   _____

_____   _____   _____

_____   _____   _____

List I-31
(Schwa Sound)
(/ile/ pronounced /əl/)
The sound /i/ as spelled and pronounced in the word

"hostile"

tile   hostile

My Words... _____   _____

_____   _____   _____

_____   _____   _____

List I-32
(Schwa Sound)
(/ion/ pronounced /ən/)
The sound /i/ as spelled and pronounced in the words

"addition" and "million"

---

gion   region, religion
hion   cushion, fashion, parishioner, passion
lion   battalion, billion, million, stallion, trillion, zillion
nion   bunion, onion
sion   collision, commission, emission, fission, fusion, mission
tion   addition, commotion, lotion, nation, position, question, ration, repetition, vision

My Words...

decision

List I-33
(Schwa Sound)
(/ior/ pronounced /yər/)
The sound /i/ as spelled and pronounced in the words

"behavior" and "savior"

---

vior   behavior, savior

My Words...

(Schwa Sound)
(/ious/ pronounced /əs/)
The sound /i/ as spelled and pronounced in the words

"ambitious" and "religious"

ious   ambitious, gracious, religious spacious, superstitious

My Words...

List I-35
(Schwa Sound)
(/ir/ pronounced /ər/)
The sound /i/ as spelled and pronounced in the word

"admirable"

ir   admirable

My Words...

List I-36
(Schwa Sound)
(/ium/ pronounced /əm/)
The sound /i/ as spelled and pronounced in the words

"Belgium" and "conundrum"

um   Belgium, conundrum

My Words...

_____   _____

_____   _____   _____

_____   _____   _____

List I-37
(Schwa Sound)
(/ius/ pronounced /əs/ or /yəs/)
The sound /i/ as spelled and pronounced in the words

"Confucius" and "genius"

ius   Confucius, genius

My Words...

_____   _____

_____   _____   _____

_____   _____   _____

List I-38
(silent /i/)
The letter /i/ as spelled and pronounced in the word

"business" and "platinum"

---

in   business, platinum

My Words...   _____   _____

_____   _____   _____

_____   _____   _____

List J-1
(/j/ pronounced /j/)

---

ja   jab, jag, jam, jar, jaw, jazz
je   Jeff, jet
ji   jib, jiffy, jig, Jill, jip
jo   job, job, jolly, jot

My Words...   _____   _____

_____   _____   _____

_____   _____   _____

_____   _____   _____

List K-1
(/k/ pronounced /k/)

k	trek
ka	kangaroo, karate, kayak
ke	keep, kennel, kernel, ketchup, key
ki	kid, kidney, kill, kind, king, kitchen, kitten
ko	koala, Koran, kosher
kr	kraken, Kremlin, krill
ku	kudos, Kuwait, kumquat

My Words...

_____ _____ _____

_____ _____ _____

_____ _____ _____

_____ _____ _____

List K-2
(/kk/ pronounced /k/)

kke	trekked
kki	trekking

My Words...

_____ _____ _____

_____ _____ _____

_____ _____ _____

List K-3
(silent /k/)

kna	knack, knapsack, knave
kne	knead, knee, knell, knew
kni	knife, knight, knit
kno	knob, knock, knoll, knot, know
knu	knuckle

My Words...

know _____ _____ _____

_____ _____ _____

List L-1
(/l/ pronounced /l/)

la	lab, lad, lag, land, lap, lard, lass, law
le	led, left, leg, lemon, lend, less, let
li	lid, lift, lip, list, lit
lo	lob, loft, log, lost
lu	lug, lung

My Words...

_____ _____ _____

_____ _____ _____

List L-2

(/le/ pronounced /əl/)
The sound /le/ as spelled and pronounced in the words

"jingle" and "people"

gle   mingle, jingle, tingle, single
ple   nipple, people, pimple

My Words...

List L-3
(/ll/ pronounced /l/)

ll   all, bell, ill, bull, pull, skull, small

lla   allay, cellar, dollar, llama, lullaby, stellar

lle   allegro, allergy, alley, collect, college, excellent, miller, seller, pellet. trolley

lli   alliance, alliteration, brilliant, chilliness, collie, million, scallion

llm   installment

lln   illness

llo   allow, billow, cello, fellow, follow, pillow, swallow, yellow

llp   smallpox

llu   allude, allure, allusion, callus, illusion, pollution

lly   belly, chilly, dolly, folly, holly, jelly, silly

My Words...

finally

pulled

List L-4
(silent /l/)

ld	could, should, would
lf	calf, half
lk	folk, polka, talk, walk, yolk
lm	almond, balm calm, palm, salmon
lv	halves, salves

My Words...

_____   _____   _____

_____   _____   _____

_____   _____   _____

_____   _____   _____

List M-1
(/m/ pronounced /m/)

ma	mad, mall, man, map, mat
me	me, medic, melt, men, mess, met
mi	mill, mind, miss, mist
mo	mob, mom, mop, moss
mu	mud, mug, mull, must

My Words...

_____   _____   _____

_____   _____   _____

_____   _____   _____

_____   _____   _____

List M-2
(/mb/ pronounced /m/)

mb   bomb, comb, climb, limb, plumber, thumb, tomb, womb

My Words...

_____

_____

_____

List M-3
(/mm/ pronounced /m/)

mma   comma, command, flammable, roommate, scrimmage
mme   commence, dammed, drummer, hammer, immense
mmi   commission, commit, summit
mmo   ammonia, common, immobile, persimmon
mmu   ammunition, communicate, immune
                mmy   dummy, mummy

My Words...

_____

_____

_____

_____

List M-4
(/mn/ pronounced /m/)

___

mn   hymn

My Words...

___

List M-5
(silent /m/)

___

mn   mnemonic

My Words...

List N-1
(/n/ pronounced /n/)

na	nab, nag, name, nap
ne	Ned, need, nest, net, new, next
ni	nifty, nip
no	nod, not, now

My Words...

_____ _____ _____

_____ _____ _____

_____ _____ _____

_____ _____ _____

List N-2
(/ng/ pronounced /ng/)

ing	ding, fling, ping, ring, sing, tingle, thing, wing

My Words...

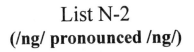

115

List N-3
(/nn/ pronounced /n/)

nna	annalist, manna, inner, pinnacle
nne	annex, banner, channel, connect, dinner, kennel
nni	canning, cannon, fanning, pinning, running
nno	announce, annoy, innocent
nnk	innkeeper
nnu	annual, annul
nny	bonny, funny, ninny, penny, runny

My Words...

_____ _____ _____

_____ _____ _____

_____ _____ _____

_____ _____ _____

_____ _____ _____

_____ _____ _____

_____ _____ _____

_____ _____ _____

_____ _____ _____

_____ _____ _____

_____ _____ _____

_____ _____ _____

_____ _____ _____

List O-1

(/ō/ with no silent /e/ ending)
The sound /o/ as spelled and pronounced in the words

"old" and "so"

---

o	banjo, go, going, no, piano, so
oa	cocoa **(Also See List O-10)**
ob	adobe, robot
oc	grocery, local, vocal
od	odor, dodo, modal, soda
oe	poem
of	gofer, sofa, tofu
og	bogey, bogus, loganberry, logo, toga, vogue
oh	Bohemia, Johan, mohair, oh, Ohio
oj	dojo, sojourn
ok	broken, broker, joker, Oklahoma, okra, poker, woken yokel
ol	old, bold, cold, fold, folk, gold, hold, mold, poll, roll, consol, told, toll, yolk
om	coma, comb, domain, moment, nomad, omen, Roman
on	only, donate, erroneous, harmonious, tonality
oo	cooperate, zoology
op	copious, dopier, gopher, loping, moping, opal, open, oral, roping
oqu	coquet, croquet, loquacious
os	ghost, gross, host, most, post, rosy
ot	both, doting, hotel, quota, rotund, totem, voting
ou	**See List O-23**
ov	clover, oval, over, rover, roving, woven
ow	**See List O-31**
oz	cozy, dozing, frozen

My Words...

_____   _____   _____

_____   _____   _____

_____   _____   _____

_____   _____   _____

_____   _____   _____

_____   _____   _____

List O-2
(/ō/ with a silent /e/ ending)
The sound /o/ as spelled and pronounced in the words

"globe" and "pore"

---

ob	globe, lobe, probe
od	abode, mode, node, rode
oe	doe, foe, hoe, oboe, potatoes, roe, toe, vetoes, woe, zeroes
og	rogue, vogue
ok	bloke, broke, woke
ol	dole, hole, mole, pole, vole
om	chrome, dome, gnome, home, tome
on	alone, bone, crone, drone, hone, lone, phone
op	cope, dope, grope, hope, mope, pope, rope
or	bore, core, gore, lore, more, pore, tore, wore
os	chose, close, pose, rose, suppose
ot	dote, quote, rote, tote, vote
ov	clove, drove, grove, rove, wove
oz	froze

My Words...

List O-3
(/o/ pronounced /ōō/ with no silent /e/ ending)
The sound /o/ as spelled and pronounced in the words

"do" and "tomb"

---

o   do, to, who
od   today
og   together
om   tomb, tomorrow, whom, womb

My Words...

List O-4
(/o/ pronounced /o͞o/ with a silent /e/ ending)
The sound /o/ as spelled and pronounced in the words

"canoe" and "move"

oe   canoe, shoe
ose   lose, whose
ove   move, prove

My Words...

List O-5
(/o/ pronounced /ŏ/)
The sound /o/ as spelled and pronounced in the words

"body" and "oxygen"

---

ob	bob, cob, gobs, gobble, hobble, lob, mob, rob, robin, sob, wobble
oc	octagon, block, crock, doctor, hockey, jock, lock, mock, rock, sock
od	odd, body, cod, fodder, god, model, modular, nod, pod, rod, sod, toddy
og	bog, boggle, cog, fog, frog, goggle, hog, jog, log, logarithm, noggin, soggy, toggle
ok	wok
ol	olive, abolish, collar, doll, golly, holly, jolly, modify, solid, volume
om	bomb, domino, hominy, mom, pompom, tomboy, zombie
on	on, ontology, bond, fond, tarragon, demon, nonpareil, ponder
op	opulent, bop, cop, crop, fop, hop, lopsided, mop, sop, top, topple
or	sorry
os	ostracize, ostrich, gosling, jostle, nostril, possible, roster
ot	otter, bottle, cot, dot, got, hot, jot, lot, mottled, pot, rot, sot, tot
ov	proverb
ow	knowledge
ox	box, fox, noxious, ox, oxygen, pox

My Words...

tomorrow

121

List O-6
(/o/ pronounced /o͝o/)
The sound /o/ as spelled and pronounced in the words

"wolf" and "woman"

ol	wolf
om	woman
or	Worcester
os	bosom

My Words... _____ _____

_____ _____ _____

_____

List O-7
(/o/ pronounced /ŭ/)
The sound /o/ as spelled and pronounced in the words

"come" and "from"

of	of
om	come, comfort, from, some stomach
on	done, honey, money, none, one, ton, tongue, won, wonder
ot	brother, mother, nothing, other
ov	cover, dove, hover, love

My Words... _____ _____

_____ _____ _____

_____ _____ _____

List O-8
(/o/ pronounced /ô/)
The sound /o/ as spelled and pronounced in the words

"dog" and "gone"

---

of	scoff
og	dog
on	gone
os	boss, cross, floss, lost, moss, toss

My Words...

List O-9
(/o/ pronounced /w/)
The sound /o/ as spelled and pronounced in the words

"once" and "one"

---

oi	choir, memoir
on	once, one

My Words...

List O-10

(/oa/ pronounced /ō/)

The sound /o/ as spelled and pronounced in the words

"boat" and "soar"

---

oac	approach, broach, coach, encroach, roach
oad	goad, load, road, toad
oaf	loaf, oaf
oag	hoagie
oak	cloak, croak, oak, soak
oal	coal, foal, goal, shoal
oam	foam, loam
oan	groan, moan
oap	soap
oar	boar, coarse, oar, roar, soar
oat	boat, coat, goat, oat, moat
oax	coax, hoax

My Words...

_____   _____   _____

_____   _____   _____

_____   _____   _____

_____   _____   _____

_____   _____   _____

_____   _____   _____

_____   _____   _____

_____   _____   _____

_____   _____   _____

List O-11
(/oa/ pronounced /ô/)
The sound /o/ as spelled and pronounced in the word

"broad"

---

oad   abroad, broad

My Words...

List O-12
(/oi/)
The sound /o/ as spelled and pronounced in the words

"coin" and "soil"

---

oid   avoid, void
oil   foil, oil, soil
oin   coin, join

My Words...

List O-13
(/ol/ pronounced /ûr/)
The sound /o/ as spelled and pronounced in the word

"colonel"

---

ol   colonel

My Words...

_____   _____   _____

_____   _____   _____

List O-14
(/ong/ pronounced /ông/)
The sound /o/ as spelled and pronounced in the words

"long" and "song"

---

on   belong, gong, long, song, wrong

My Words...

List O-15
(/oo/ pronounced /ō/)
The sound /o/ as spelled and pronounced in the words

"door" and "poor"

oor   door, floor, poor

My Words...

_____ _____

_____ _____ _____

_____ _____ _____

List O-16
(/oo/ pronounced /o͞o/ with no silent /e/ ending)
The sound /o/ as spelled and pronounced in the words

"food" and "tool"

ooc	pooch
ood	brood, food, mood
oof	poof
ool	cool, fool, pool, stool, tool
oom	room
oon	boon
oop	droop
oot	boot, toot

My Words...

_____ _____

_____ _____

_____ _____

_____ _____

_____ _____

_____ _____

List O-17
(/oo/ pronounced /o͞o/ with a silent /e/ ending)
The sound /o/ as spelled and pronounced in the words

"caboose" and "loose"

oose   caboose, choose, goose, loose

My Words...

_____ _____ _____

_____ _____ _____

_____ _____ _____

List O-18
(/oo/ pronounced /o͝o/)
The sound /o/ as spelled and pronounced in the words

"wood" and "wool"

od   good, hood, stood, wood
of   hoof
og   boogie
ok   book, cook, cookie, hook, look, nook, rook, took
ol   wool

My Words...

_____ _____ _____

_____ _____ _____

_____ _____ _____

List O-19
(/oo/ pronounced /ŭ/)
The sound /o/ as spelled and pronounced in the words

"blood" and "flood"

ood   blood, flood

My Words...

_____   _____   _____

_____   _____   _____

_____   _____   _____

_____   _____   _____

List O-20
(/or/ pronounced /ôr/)
The sound /o/ as spelled and pronounced in the words

"coral" and "port"

or   boring, cord, for, goring, lord, morbid, or, orb, orchid, order, port, sport

My Words...

_____   _____   _____

_____   _____   _____

_____   _____   _____

List O-21
(/or/ pronounced /ûr/)
The sound /o/ as spelled and pronounced in the words

"word" and "work"

---

or   word, work, worse

My Words... _____ _____

_____ _____ _____

_____ _____ _____

List O-22
(/ou/)
The sound /o/ as spelled and pronounced in the words

"loud" and "proud"

---

oub	doubt
ouc	couch, ouch
oud	aloud, cloud, loud
ough	drought, plough
oun	abound, around, bound, found, hound, mound, noun, pound, round, sound
our	flour, hour, our, sour
ous	thousand
out	out, about, devout, grout, hour, lout, mouth, pout, rout

My Words... _____ _____

_____ _____ _____

_____ _____ _____

List O-23
(/ou/ pronounced /ō/)
The sound /o/ as spelled and pronounced in the words

"boulder" and "shoulder"

oul   boulder, shoulder, soul

My Words...
_____ _____

_____ _____ _____

_____ _____ _____

List O-24
(/ou/ pronounced /ōo/)
The sound /o/ as spelled and pronounced in the words

"through" and "rendezvous"

ou   you
oug   through
our   tour
ous   couscous, rendezvous
out   route

My Words...
_____ _____

_____ _____ _____

_____ _____ _____

List O-25

(/ou/ pronounced /ŏ/)

The sound /o/ as spelled and pronounced in the word

"Gloucester"

ouc   Gloucester

My Words...

_____   _____   _____

_____   _____   _____

_____   _____   _____

List O-26

(/ou/ pronounced /o͝o/)

The sound /o/ as spelled and pronounced in the words

"would" and "could"

ou   could, should, would

My Words...

_____   _____   _____

_____   _____   _____

_____   _____   _____

_____   _____   _____

List O-27
(/ou/ pronounced /ŭ/)
The sound /o/ as spelled and pronounced in the words

"double" and "trouble"

---

oub	double, trouble
ouc	touch
ough	rough
oun	young

My Words...

_____ _____ _____

_____ _____ _____

_____ _____ _____

List O-28
(/ough/ pronounced /ô/)
The sound /o/ as spelled and pronounced in the words

"bought" and "thought"

---

ou   bought, brought, fought, ought, sought, thought

My Words...

_____ _____ _____

_____ _____ _____

_____ _____ _____

List O-29
(/our/ pronounced /ôr/)
The sound /o/ as spelled and pronounced in the words

"court" and "pour"

our   course, court, pour, source

My Words...

_____   _____

_____   _____   _____

_____   _____   _____

_____   _____   _____

List O-30
(/our/ pronounced /ûr/)
The sound /o/ as spelled and pronounced in the words

"courage" and "courtesy"

our   courage, courtesy, journey, scourge

My Words...

_____   _____

_____   _____   _____

_____   _____   _____

_____   _____   _____

List O-31
(/ow/ pronounced /ō/)
The sound /o/ as spelled and pronounced in the words

"bowl" and "own"

bow	bowl
dow	window
low	fallow, follow, low, swallow, tallow, yellow
now	know
row	arrow, grow, grown, row

My Words...

tomorrow

List O-32
(/ow/ pronounced /ou/)
The sound /o/ as spelled and pronounced in the words

"crowd" and "power"

ow   bow (as in the bow *of a ship*), cow, howl, now, owl, plow, power, tower, trowel, vowel

My Words...

List O-33
(/oy/ pronounced /oi/)
The sound /o/ as spelled and pronounced in the words

"employ" and "enjoy"

---

boy	boy, boyish
coy	coy
joy	enjoy, joy
loy	employ, ploy
noy	annoy
roy	royal
soy	soy
toy	toy
voy	convoy

My Words...

List O-34
(Schwa Sound)
(/o/ pronounced /ə/)
The sound "o" as spelled and pronounced in the words

"official" and "commit"
(Note: For schwa sounds that involve the letter /i/, see the Word Lists for I-21 through I-27)

ob	oblige, obligatory, obliterate, observe, obstruction, obtain
oc	bullock, hassock, havoc
od	method
of	offend, official
og	apology, hydrogen, nitrogen
oi	connoisseur, porpoise
ol	idol, symbol
on	bacon, cannon, colony, color, confuse, connect, lemon, lion, reason, reckon, second, sermon
om	atom, commit, comply, compose, kingdom, ransom
op	envelop, Europe
os	purpose
ot	pilot, pivot, riot
ou	fabulous, marvelous, mischievous, mucous, wondrous

My Words..

_____ _____ _____

_____ _____ _____

_____ _____ _____

_____ _____ _____

_____ _____ _____

_____ _____ _____

_____ _____ _____

List O-35
(Schwa Sound)
(/or/ pronounced /ər/)
The sound /o/ as spelled and pronounced in the words

"doctor" and "sailor"

___

or   armor, color, doctor, harbor, minor, sailor, terror

My Words...   _____   _____

_____   _____   _____

_____   _____   _____

List O-36
(silent /o/)
The letter "o" as spelled and pronounced in the words

"laboratory" and "people"

___

oe   Oedipus
on   button, cotton, mutton
op   people
or   laboratory

My Words...   _____   _____

_____   _____   _____

_____   _____   _____

List P-1
(/p/ pronounced /p/)

---

pa   pack, pad, pal, Pam, pan, part
pe   peck, peg, pen, pepper, person
pi   pick, pig, pill, pig
pl   plan, plow
po   pocket, pod, pop, poor, pot
pu   pup, puppet, puppy, putrid
py   happy, jumpy, lumpy, poppy, sappy

My Words... _____ _____

_____ _____ _____

_____ _____ _____

List P-2
(/ph/ pronounced /f/)

---

pha   phantom, pharaoh, pharmacy, phase
phe   gopher, nephew, pheasant, phenomena, prophet, sphere
phi   Phil, philanthropy, philosophy
pho   phobia, phoenix, phone, phonics, photograph, phony
phy   philosophy, phylum, physician, physics

My Words... _____ _____

_____ _____ _____

_____ _____ _____

_____ _____ _____

List P-3
(/pp/ pronounced /p/)

ppa   apparel, apparent, applaud, apply, approach, approve
ppe   appeal, copper, flopped, pepper, puppet
ppi   flipping, peppiness, stopping
po   opportunity, opposite, support
ppy   guppy, happy, nippy, puppy
ppl   apply, ripple, supple

My Words...

_____ _____ _____
_____ _____ _____
_____ _____ _____
_____ _____ _____
_____ _____ _____

List P-4
(/pt/ pronounced /t/)

pt   receipt

My Words...

_____ _____ _____
_____ _____ _____

List P-5
(silent /p/)

pb   cupboard, raspberry
pn   pneumonia
ps   psalm, psychology,
pt   ptarmigan, pterodactyl

My Words...

List Q-1
(/qu/ pronounced /kw/)

qua   quality, quart, quarter, quartz
que   queen, quell, query, quest
qui   quill, quit, quiz

My Words...

List Q-2
(/qu/ pronounced /k/)

qua   quay
que   baroque, bouquet, conquer, unique

My Words...

List R-1
(/r/ pronounced /r/)

ra   radical, raft, rag, ram, ran, rap, rat, raw
re   red, regular, rest
ri   rib, rid, rig, rim, rip
ro   rob, rod
ru   rub, rug, run, rust, rut

My Words...

List R-2
(/rr/ pronounced /r/)

rra	arrange, arrest, arrive, corral, errand,
rre	barren, barrel, correct, correspond, squirrel
rrh	catarrh, diarrhea, myrrh,
rri	barrier, carrier, corridor, territory, warrior
rro	burrow, error, furrow, narrow, sorrow
rru	cirrus, corrupt,
rry	carry, ferry, flurry, scurry, tarry

My Words...

horrible _____ _____

_____ _____ _____

_____ _____ _____

List S-1
(/s/ pronounced /s/)

sa	sad, sag, Sam, sand, sap, sat, saw, say
se	see, sell, send, set
si	sift, silly, sin, sip, sister, sit
so	sob, sod, soft, soggy, son, sop
su	sub, suffer, sun, supper
sw	swab, swat, swig, swill, switch

My Words...

_____ _____ _____

_____ _____ _____

_____ _____ _____

List S-2
(/s/ pronounced /sh/ and /zh/)

si	vision
ssi	fission, fissure, mission
su	casual, measure, pleasure, usual

My Words...

_____ _____ _____

_____ _____ _____

_____ _____ _____

_____ _____ _____

List S-3
(/s/ pronounced /z/)

as	laser
es	fries, lies, pies, ties, toes, result
is	poison, rise, surprise, wise
os	close (*verb*), hose, loser, mosey, nose, pose, rose
se	surmise, surprise, wise
us	business, busy
yes	dyes
ys	boys, days, guys, plays, rays, says, ways

My Words...

_____ _____ _____

_____ _____ _____

_____ _____ _____

_____ _____ _____

List S-4
(/sc/ pronounced /s/)

---

sc   abscess, adolescent, ascent, reminisce

My Words...

_____   _____

_____   _____   _____

_____   _____   _____

_____   _____   _____

_____   _____   _____

_____   _____

List S-5
(/sh/ pronounced /sh/)

---

sha   shabby, shaft, shag, shall, sham, shark
she   shed, shell, shepherd
shi   shift, shim, shin, ship, shirt
sho   shod, shop, shore, shot, shove, show
shr   shrank, shrink, shrunk

My Words...

_____   _____

_____   _____   _____

_____   _____   _____

_____   _____   _____

List S-6
(/ss/ pronounced /s/)

ss   brass, crass, cross, dress, fuss, lass, mass, pass
ssa   assassin, massacre, massage
sse   assemble, assert, crevasse, dessert, possess, vessel
ssi   assassin, assignment, classic, dissipate, pessimist, pressing
sso   assorted, dissonant, dissolve
ssu   assume
ssy   mossy
ssl   hassle, tassel

My Words...

possible

List S-7
(/sw/ pronounced /s/)

---

sw   sword, *answer*

My Words...

answer _____   _____   _____

_____   _____   _____

_____   _____   _____

_____   _____   _____

List S-8
(silent /s/)

---

ps   corps, debris, island, isle

My Words...

_____   _____   _____

_____   _____   _____

_____   _____   _____

_____   _____   _____

_____   _____   _____

List T-1
(/t/ pronounced /t/)

ta	tab, tad, tag, tall, tan, tap, tar
te	Ted, tell, ten, test
ti	tick, tiff, Tim, tin, tip
to	to, Todd, Tom, ton, top, toss, tot
tu	tub, tug

shant
slant
ant
pant
nant
want

My Words...

instantly

List T-2
(/tt/ pronounced /t/)

tta	attack, attain, cottage
tte	attempt, butter, corvette, critter, hotter, litter, matter, splatter, written
tti	attic, fitting, hitting, quitting, potting
tto	attorney, bottom, cotton
ttr	attract, attribute
ttu	attune
tty	batty, patty, pretty, ratty
ttl	brittle, cattle, kettle, little, rattle, tattle

My Words...

spaghetti
pretty

List T-3
(/t/ pronounced /ch/)

te   righteous
ti   Christian, question
tu   actual, mature, nature, picture, sanctuary, virtue

My Words...

List T-4
(/t/ pronounced /sh/)
(See also Lists I-32 and I-34)

tion   action, diction, fiction, lotion, motion, nation, notion, portion, ration, sensation

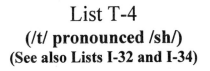

My Words...

List T-5
(/th/ pronounced /th/)

tha	that
the	the, their, there, these
thi	thin, think, this
tho	those, thought
thr	threw, throw

My Words...

List T-6
(silent /t/)

---

ot   depot
st   fasten, hasten, listen, soften, whistle

My Words...

_____   _____

_____   _____   _____

_____   _____   _____

List U-1
(/u/ pronounced /o͞o/ with no silent /e/ ending)
The sound /u/ as spelled and pronounced in the words

"ruby" and "unit"

---

u	flu
ua	casual, dual, duality, gradual, mutual
ub	ruby
uc	cuckoo, Lucas
ud	Judaism, Judy, nudity, student
ue	duel, duet, cruel **(See Also List U-18)**
ui	ruin **(See Also List U-21)**
ul	duly, truly
um	numeral, puma, sumo, tumor
un	lunar, unit
uo	buoy, duo
up	super
ur	rural
us	Susan
ut	duty, truth

My Words...

situated

151

List U-2
(/u/ pronounced /o͞o/ with a silent /e/ ending)
The sound /u/ as pronounced in the words

"tube" and "dune"

---

ub	tube
uc	deduce, produce, reduce
ud	dude, etude, nude, rude
ue	due, glue, rue, true, Tuesday **(See Also List U-18)**
uk	fluke
ul	rule
um	assume, consume, costume
un	dune, June, prune, rune, tune
up	dupe, duplicate, scruple
ur	endure, lure, manure
ut	chute, flute, lute

My Words...

List U-3
(/u/ pronounced /yo͞o/ with no silent /e/ ending)
The sound /u/ as spelled and pronounced in the words

"fury" and "putrid"

---

un	union
us	usual
bu	abusing
cu	cucumber, cumulus, curing
fu	fuel, fury
hu	hubris, humidify, humidor, humility, humongous, humor
mu	communicator, emu, impunity, mule, music, tunic, union, unit
nu	annual, Inuit
pu	puberty, pupil, purify, putrid
uu	**See List U-25**

My Words...

List U-4
(/u/ pronounced /yōō/ with a silent /e/ ending)
The sound /u/ as spelled and pronounced in the words

"bugle" and "hue"

u	use
bu	abuse, bugle, butane, rebuke
cu	cube, cue, cumulative, cute
fu	confuse, fuse, refuse
gu	argue
hu	hue
lu	volume
mu	mule, mute
pu	puke, punitive

My Words...

_____ _____ _____

_____ _____ _____

_____ _____ _____

_____ _____ _____

_____ _____ _____

_____ _____ _____

_____ _____ _____

_____ _____ _____

_____ _____ _____

_____ _____ _____

_____ _____ _____

List U-5
(/ŭ/ with no silent /e/ ending)
The letter /u/ as pronounced in the words

"buffalo" and "stuff"

ub	cub, dub, grub, hub, nub, pub, publish, rubber
uc	buck, duck, duct, luck, much, muck, puck, such, tuck
ud	buddy, cud, cudgel, dud, mud, suds
uf	buffer, cuff, fluff, huff, muff, puff, suffer
ug	ugly, bug, dug, hug, lug, mug, put, rug, tug
ul	annul, difficult, sullen
um	bum, clumsy, drum, gum, hum, jump, lump, number, plumber, rum, summer
un	abundant, fun, gun, hundred, hung, hunger, sun, under
up	disrupt, erupt, guppy, nuptial, puppy, supper, up, upper
us	bus, custard, dust, fuss, gusto, hustle, just, luster, mustard, pus, rust, sustain, trust
ut	utter, but, butter, cut, cutlass, Dutch, gut, gutter, hut, jut, mutter, nut, putter, rut
ux	flux, tuxedo
uz	buzz, fuzz, fuzzy

My Words...

155

List U-6
(/ŭ/ with a silent /e/ ending)
The sound /u/ as spelled and pronounced in the words

"budge" and "subtle"

---

ub	bubble, budge, rubble, sludge
ud	huddle, muddle, puddle, subtle
uf	ruffle
ul	ultimate
un	uncle, bundle, jungle, plunge
ux	deluxe
uz	guzzle, huddle, muzzle, puzzle

My Words...

_____   _____

_____   _____   _____

_____   _____   _____

_____   _____   _____

List U-7
(/u/ pronounced /ä/)
The sound /u/ as pronounced in the word

"guard"

---

ua	guard, guarded, guardian, guarding

My Words...

_____   _____

_____   _____   _____

List U-8
(/u/ pronounced /ě/)
The sound /u/ as spelled and pronounced in the word

"bury"

---

ury   bury

My Words...

    buried

List U-9
(/u/ pronounced /ĭ/)
The sound /u/ as pronounced in the words

"busy" and "business"

---

us   busy, business
ut   minute

My Words...

List U-10
(/u/ pronounced /ôr/)
The sound /u/ as spelled and pronounced in the word

"quarantine" and "quarry"

---

uar   quarantine, quarry

My Words...

List U-11
(/u/ pronounced /o͝o/ with no silent /e/ ending)
The sound /u/ as pronounced in the words

"full" and "put"

---

ud	pudding
ug	sugar
ul	bull, bullet, full, July, pulpit, pull, pulley
ur	rural
us	push
ut	butcher, put, putting

My Words...

List U-12
(/u/ pronounced /o͝o/ with a silent /e/ ending)
The sound /u/ as spelled and produced in the words

"endure" and "sure"

ure   endure, ensure, pressure, rupture, sure

My Words...

_____ _____ _____

_____ _____ _____

_____ _____ _____

_____ _____ _____

List U-13
(/ur/ pronounced /ûr/)
The sound /u/ as spelled and pronounced in the words

"fur" and "jury"

ur   burlap, church, cur, curl, fur, furnace, hurl, jury, murder, murky, purge, surf, surge, turf, turkey

My Words...

_____ _____ _____

_____ _____ _____

_____ _____ _____

_____ _____ _____

List U-14

(/u/ pronounced /w/)
The sound /u/ as spelled and pronounced in the words

"guano" and "languish"

---

gua   language, guano, guava
gui   languid, languish
qu   **See List Q-1**
su   dissuade, persuade, suede, suite

My Words...

_____ _____

_____ _____ _____

_____ _____ _____

_____ _____ _____

List U-15

(/u/ pronounced /yōo/ with a silent /e/ ending)
The sound /u/ as spelled and pronounced in the words

"cure" and "demure"

---

ure   cure, demure, pure

My Words...

_____ _____

_____ _____ _____

_____ _____ _____

List U-16
(/ua/ pronounced /ă/)
The sound /u/ as spelled and pronounced in the word

"guarantee"

uar   guarantee

My Words...

List U-17
(/ue/ pronounced /ĕ/)
The sound /u/ as spelled and pronounced in the words

"guess" and "guest"

gue   guess, guest

My Words...

List U-18
(/ue/ pronounced /ōō/)
The sound /u/ as spelled and pronounced in the words

"blue" and "Tuesday"

---

ue   blue
ues   Tuesday

My Words...

List U-19
(/ui/ pronounced /ē/)
The sound /u/ as spelled and pronounced in the word

"mosquito"

---

qui   mosquito

My Words...

List U-20
(/ui/ pronounced /ī/)
The sound /u/ as spelled and pronounced in the word

"guide"

uid   guide

My Words...

List U-21
(/ui/ pronounced /o͞o/ with no silent /e/ ending)
The sound /u/ as spelled and pronounced in the words

"fruit" and "suit"

ui   fruit, suit

My Words...

List U-22
(/ui/ pronounced /o͞o/ with a silent /e/ ending)
The sound /u/ as spelled and pronounced in the words

"bruise" and "cruise"

uis   bruise, cruise, nuisance

My Words...

_____ _____
_____ _____ _____
_____ _____ _____
_____ _____ _____

List U-23
(/ui/ pronounced /ĭ/)
The sound /u/ as spelled and pronounced in the words

"biscuit" and "circuit"

uil   build, built, guild, guilt
uit   biscuit, circuit, guitar

My Words...

_____ _____
_____ _____ _____
_____ _____ _____
_____ _____ _____

List U-24
(/uo/ pronounced /oi/)
The sound /u/ as spelled and pronounced in the words

"buoyancy" and "buoyant"

uoy   buoyancy, buoyant

My Words...

List U-25
(/uu/ pronounced /yo͞o/)
The sound /u/ as spelled and pronounced in the word

"vacuum"

uum   vacuum

My Words...

List U-26
(/uy/ pronounced /ī/)
The sound /u/ as spelled and pronounced in the words

"buy" and "guy"

---

uy   buy, guy

My Words...   _____   _____

_____   _____   _____

List U-27
(Schwa Sound)
(/u/ pronounced /ə/)
The sound /u/ as spelled and pronounced in the words

"asparagus" and "buffoon"

---

ub	cherub, subdue, sublime, submit
uc	educate, lettuce, successor
uf	buffet, buffoon
ug	suggest, suggestion
ul	calculus, careful, consul, faithful, manipulate, peninsula, scapula, undulate
um	auditorium, calcium, cranium, linoleum, petroleum, podium, quantum, sanctum
un	voluntary
up	support
ur	caricature, conjecture, future, lecture, picture, puncture, pressure, rapture, Saturn
us	asparagus, cactus, campus, circus, focus, industry, Leviticus, mollusk, opus
ut	attributive, gamut, halibut, salutation

My Words...   _____   _____

_____   _____   _____

_____   _____   _____

List U-28
(Schwa Sound)
(/ue/ pronounced /əe/)
The sound /u/ as spelled and pronounced in the word

"guerilla"

---

uer   guerilla

My Words...

_____   _____

_____   _____   _____

_____   _____   _____

List U-29
(Schwa Sound)
(/ul/ pronounced /əl/)
The sound /u/ as spelled and pronounced in the words

"awful" and "faculty"

---

cul   faculty
ful   awful, careful, cheerful, earful

My Words...

_____   _____

_____   _____   _____

_____   _____   _____

_____   _____   _____

List U-30
(Schwa Sound)
(/uor/ pronounced /ər/)
The sound /u/ as spelled and pronounced in the word

"languor"

uor   languor

My Words...

_____

List U-31
(Schwa Sound)
(/ur/pronounced /ər/)
The sound /u/ as spelled and pronounced in the words

"leisure" and "verdure"

ure   azure, failure, future, injure, leisure, picture, Saturday, verdure

My Words...

List U-32
(silent /u/)
The letter /u/ as spelled and pronounced in the words

"synagogue" and "tongue"

ua	victual
gue	fatigue, fugue, meringue, morgue, Prague, synagogue, rogue, tongue, vague, vogue
que	antique, boutique, plaque, mosque, technique

My Words..

_____ _____ _____

_____ _____ _____

_____ _____ _____

_____ _____ _____

List V-1
(/v/ pronounced /v/)

va	valid, valor, van, valve
ve	velvet, vendor, venison, verb
vi	vial, vice, victim, video
vo	volume, vomit, vortex, vote
vu	vulgar, vulnerable, vulture

My Words..

_____ _____ _____

_____ _____ _____

_____ _____ _____

List V-2
(/vv/ pronounced /v/)

vvi   revving

My Words...		

List W-1
(/w/ pronounced /w/)

wa	wad, wag, wall, war, was
we	we, weed, well, were, west, wet
wi	wife, wig, will, win, wit
wo	woman, wonder, wood, would

My Words...		
went		

List W-2
(/wh/ pronounced /w/)

---

wha	whale, what
whe	wheat, when, whet, whey
whi	whiff, whine, whip, whirl, white
why	why

My Words...

_____ _____ _____

_____ _____ _____

_____ _____ _____

_____ _____ _____

List W-3
(silent /w/)

---

sw	answer, boatswain, sword
tw	two
wa	gunwale
wh	who, whom, whose, whole,
wr	wrack, wrap, wrath, wren, wreath, wrist, write, wrong, wrote

My Words...   wrote

_____ write

_____ _____ _____

_____ _____ _____

List X-1
(/x/ pronounced /gz/)

xie   anxiety

My Words...

_____   _____   _____

_____   _____   _____

_____   _____   _____

_____   _____   _____

List X-2
(/x/ pronounced /k/)

xio   anxious, obnoxious

My Words...

_____   _____   _____

_____   _____   _____

_____   _____   _____

_____   _____   _____

_____   _____   _____

_____   _____   _____

_____   _____   _____

List X-3
(/x/ pronounced /z/)

xe   xebec, xenon, xerography, xylem, xylophone

My Words...

_____   _____   _____

_____   _____   _____

_____   _____   _____

_____   _____   _____

_____   _____   _____

_____   _____   _____

List X-4
(silent /x/)

ix   grand prix
ux   faux pas, Sioux

My Words...

_____   _____   _____

_____   _____   _____

_____   _____   _____

List Y-1
(/y/ pronounced /y/)

---

ya   yak, yarn,
ye   year, yellow, yes
yo   yoga, yonder, York, you, your

My Words...

List Y-2
(/y/ pronounced /ē/ with no silent /e/ ending)
The sound /y/ as spelled and pronounced in the words

"family" and "silly"

by	chubby, grubby, hobby, lobby, rugby
cy	juicy, Lucy, racy
dy	body, gaudy, lady, tidy
gy	baggy biology, mangy, foggy, prodigy, psychology
ky	funky, hockey, junky, lanky
ly	daily, family, only, simply, silly, suddenly
my	chummy, dreamy, foamy, roomy
ny	any, bony, grainy, loony, phony, rainy
oy	buoy
py	choppy, happy, puppy, sappy, sloppy
ry	cavalry, country, dowry, merry, scary, worry
sy	bossy, daisy, ecstasy, messy
ty	city, gritty, pantry, party, pity, pretty, tasty, thrifty, witty
vy	gravy, heavy, ivy, wavy
wy	showy
xy	boxy, foxy, proxy, waxy
zy	crazy, hazy, lazy

To add an ending such as ed, ing, ness, es change the y to i

My Words...

duties

List Y-3
(/y/ as /ī/ with no silent /e/ ending)
The sound /y/ as spelled and pronounced in the words

"sky" and "by"

ay	ay, kayak
by	by, bypass
cy	cyan, Cyclops, cypress
dy	dying, dynamic
ey	eying
gy	Argyll, gyroscope
hy	hyper, hypothesis, shyest, why
ky	sky
ly	fly, imply, multiply, plywood, rely, reply, supply
my	my
ny	nylon
py	pylon
ry	cry, dryer, pry, Ryan
ty	sty, tycoon, typhoon, tyrant
vy	vying
wy	Wyoming
zy	zydeco

My Words...

_____ _____ _____

_____ _____ _____

_____ _____ _____

_____ _____ _____

_____ _____ _____

_____ _____ _____

_____ _____ _____

_____ _____ _____

List Y-4
(/y/ pronounced /ī/ with a silent /e/ ending)
The sound /y/ as spelled and pronounced in the words

"bye" and "rye"

---

ay	aye
by	bye, byline, byte
cy	cycle
dy	dye, dynamite
ey	eye
hy	rhyme, thyme
ly	acolyte, lye, paralyze
py	pyre
ry	rye
ty	style, type
xy	xylophone
zy	enzyme

My Words...

List Y-5
(/y/ pronounced /ĭ/)
The sound /y/ as spelled and pronounced in the words

"syncopate" and "gypsum"

cy	bicycle, cyclical, cyst
dy	dysfunction
gy	gypsy, gypsum
hy	hypocrite, rhythm,
ly	cataclysm, lynx
my	myth
ny	antonym, homonym, synonym
py	pygmy
ry	gryphon, larynx
sy	syllable, symbol, syncopate, system
ty	typical
xy	oxygen

My Words...

_____   _____   _____

_____   _____   _____

_____   _____   _____

_____   _____   _____

_____   _____   _____

_____   _____   _____

_____   _____   _____

_____   _____   _____

_____   _____   _____

_____   _____   _____

List Y-6
(/y/ pronounced /îr/)
The sound /y/ as spelled and pronounced in the words

"syrup" and "pyramid"

lyr	lyric
pyr	pyramid
syr	syrup
tyr	tyranny, tyrannical

My Words...

_____ _____ _____

_____ _____ _____

_____ _____ _____

List Y-7
(/y/ pronounced /îr/)
The sound /y/ as spelled and pronounced in the words

"Kyrie" and "Syria"

kyr	Kyrie
myr	myriad
pyr	Pyrenees
syr	Syracuse, Syria, syrinx

My Words...

_____ _____ _____

_____ _____ _____

_____ _____ _____

(/y/ pronounced /ûr/)
The sound /y/ as spelled and pronounced in the words

"myrrh" and "myrtle"

myr   myrrh, myrtle

My Words...

List Y-9
(Schwa Sound)
(/y/ pronounced /ə/)
The sound /y/ as spelled and pronounced in the words

"misogyny" and "uranyl"

dy   adynamia
gy   misogyny
ny   uranyl

My Words...

List Y-10
(Schwa Sound)
(/yr/ pronounced /ər/)
The sound /y/ as spelled and pronounced in the words

"martyr" and "zephyr"

hyr   zephyr
tyr   martyr, satyr

My Words...

_____   _____   _____

_____   _____   _____

_____   _____   _____

_____   _____   _____

List Z-1
(/z/ pronounced /z/)

za   zany, zap
ze   zero, zest
zi   zinc, zip
zo   zone, zoo

My Words...

_____   _____   _____

_____   _____   _____

_____   _____   _____

_____   _____   _____

List Z-2
(/zz/ pronounced /z/)

---

zzy   dizzy, fuzzy, tizzy
zzl   dazzle, guzzle, nozzle, puzzle, sizzle

My Words...

List Z-3
(silent /z/)

---

ez   laissez-faire, rendezvous

My Words...